From Michelle
Y0-EBB-436

♍ LOVE SIGNS ♍

VIRGO
August 24 – September 22

JULIA & DEREK PARKER

Dedicated to Martin Lethbridge

A DK PUBLISHING BOOK

Project Editor • Annabel Morgan
Art Editor • Anna Benjamin
Managing Editor • Francis Ritter
Managing Art Editor • Derek Coombes
DTP Designer • Cressida Joyce
Production Controller • Martin Croshaw
US Editor • Constance M. Robinson

ACKNOWLEDGMENTS

Photography: Steve Gorton: pp. 10, 13–15, 17–19, 46–49; Ian O'Leary: 16. *Additional photography by:* Colin Keates, David King, Monique Le Luhandre, David Murray, Tim Ridley, Clive Streeter, Harry Taylor, Matthew Ward. *Artworks:* Nic Demin: 34–45; Peter Lawman: *jacket*, 4, 12; Paul Redgrave: 24–33; Satwinder Sehmi: *glyphs;* Jane Thomson: *borders;* Rosemary Woods: 11.

Peter Lawman's paintings are exhibited by the Portal Gallery Ltd, London.

Picture credits: Bridgeman Art Library/Hermitage, St. Petersburg: 51; Robert Harding Picture Library: 20l, 20c, 20r; Images Colour Library: 9; The National Gallery, London: 11; Tony Stone Images: 21t, 21b; The Victoria and Albert Museum, London: 5; Zefa: 21c.

First American Edition, 1996
2 4 6 8 10 9 7 5 3 1

Published in the United States by
DK Publishing, Inc., 95 Madison Avenue, New York, New York 10016
Visit us on the World Wide Web at http://www.dk.com

Copyright © 1996 Dorling Kindersley Limited, London
Text copyright © 1996 Julia and Derek Parker

All rights reserved under International and Pan-American Copyright Conventions. No part of this publication may be reproduced, stored in a retrieval system, or transmitted in any form or by any means, electronic, mechanical, photocopying, recording, or otherwise, without the prior written permission of the copyright owner. Published in Great Britain by Dorling Kindersley Limited.
Distributed by Houghton Mifflin Company, Boston.

A catalog record is available from the Library of Congress.

ISBN 0-7894-1094-X

Reproduced by Bright Arts, Hong Kong
Printed and bound by Imago, Hong Kong

CONTENTS

Astrology & You 8

Looking for a Lover 10

You & Your Lover 12

The Food of Love 16

Places to Love 20

Venus & Mars 22

Your Love Life 24

Your Sex Life 34

Tokens of Love 46

Your Permanent Relationship 50

Venus & Mars Tables 52

ASTROLOGY & YOU

THERE IS MUCH MORE TO ASTROLOGY THAN YOUR SUN SIGN.
A SIMPLE INVESTIGATION INTO THE POSITION OF THE OTHER
PLANETS AT THE MOMENT OF YOUR BIRTH WILL PROVIDE YOU
WITH FASCINATING INSIGHTS INTO YOUR PERSONALITY.

*Y*our birth sign, or Sun sign, is the sign of the zodiac that the Sun occupied at the moment of your birth. The majority of books on astrology concentrate only on explaining the relevance of the Sun signs. This is a simple form of astrology that can provide you with some interesting but rather general information about you and your personality. In this book, we take you a step further, and reveal how the planets Venus and Mars work in association with your Sun sign to influence your attitudes toward romance and sexuality.

In order to gain a detailed insight into your personality, a "natal" horoscope, or birth chart, is necessary. This details the position of all the planets in our solar system at the moment of your birth, not just the position of the Sun. Just as the Sun occupied one of the 12 zodiac signs when you were born, perhaps making you "a Geminian" or "a Sagittarian," so each of the other planets occupied a certain sign. Each planet governs a different area of your personality, and the planets Venus and Mars are responsible for your attitudes toward love and sex, respectively.

For example, if you are a Sun-sign Sagittarian, according to the attributes of the sign you should be a dynamic, freedom-loving character. However, if Venus occupied Libra when you were born, you may make a passive and clinging partner – qualities that are supposedly completely alien to Sagittarians.

A MAP OF THE CONSTELLATION

The 16th-century astronomer Copernicus first made the revolutionary suggestion that the planets orbit the Sun rather than Earth. In this 17th-century constellation chart, the Sun is shown at the center of the solar system.

The tables on pages 52–61 of this book will enable you to discover the positions of Mars and Venus at the moment of your birth. Once you have read this information, turn to pages 22–45. On these pages we explain how the influences of Venus and Mars interact with the characteristics of your Sun sign. This information will provide you with many illuminating insights into your personality, and explains how the planets have formed your attitudes toward love and sex.

LOOKING FOR A LOVER

ASTROLOGY CAN PROVIDE YOU WITH VALUABLE INFORMATION
ON HOW TO INITIATE AND MAINTAIN RELATIONSHIPS. IT CAN
ALSO TELL YOU HOW COMPATIBLE YOU ARE WITH YOUR LOVER,
AND HOW SUCCESSFUL YOUR RELATIONSHIP IS LIKELY TO BE.

People frequently use astrology to lead into a relationship, and "What sign are you?" is often used as a conversation opener. Some people simply introduce the subject as an opening gambit, while others place great importance on this question and its answer.

Astrology can affect the way you think and behave when you are in love. It can also provide you with fascinating information about your lovers and your relationships. Astrology cannot tell you who to fall in love with or who to avoid, but it can offer you some very helpful advice.

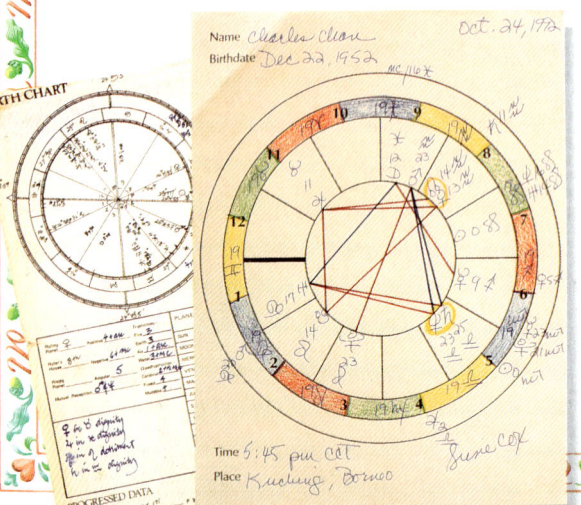

BIRTH CHARTS
Synastry involves the comparison of two people's charts in order to assess their compatibility in all areas of their relationship. The process can highlight any areas of common interest or potential conflict.

THE TABLE OF ELEMENTS
People whose signs are grouped under the same element tend to find it easy to fall into a happy relationship. The groupings are:
FIRE: *Aries, Leo, Sagittarius*
EARTH: *Taurus, Virgo, Capricorn*
AIR: *Gemini, Libra, Aquarius*
WATER: *Cancer, Scorpio, Pisces*

When you meet someone to whom you are attracted, astrology can provide you with a valuable insight into his or her personality. It may even reveal unattractive characteristics that your prospective partner is trying to conceal.

Astrologers are often asked to advise lovers involved in an ongoing relationship, or people who are contemplating a love affair. This important aspect of astrology is called synastry, and involves comparing the birth charts of the two people concerned. Each birth chart records the exact position of the planets at the moment and place of a person's birth. By interpreting each chart separately, then comparing them, an astrologer can assess the compatibility of any two people, showing where problems may arise in their relationship, and where strong bonds will form.

One of the greatest astrological myths is that people of some signs are not compatible with people of certain other signs. This is completely untrue. Whatever your Sun sign, you can have a happy relationship with a person of any other sign.

YOU & YOUR LOVER

KNOWING ABOUT YOURSELF AND YOUR LOVER IS THE KEY TO A HAPPY RELATIONSHIP. HERE WE REVEAL THE TRADITIONAL ASSOCIATIONS OF VIRGO, YOUR COMPATIBILITY WITH ALL THE SUN SIGNS, AND THE FLOWERS LINKED WITH EACH SIGN.

VIRGO RULES ALL NUT-BEARING TREES, SUCH AS THE HAZEL

MERCURY, THE PLANET OF COMMUNICATION, RULES VIRGO

SMALL FLOWERS, SUCH AS THE BUTTERCUP, ARE LINKED WITH VIRGO

VEGETABLES ARE TRADITIONALLY ASSOCIATED WITH VIRGO

DOMESTIC PETS – CATS AND DOGS IN PARTICULAR – ARE RULED BY VIRGO

VIRGOS HAVE WELL-PROPORTIONED, COMPACT BODIES

– YOU & YOUR LOVER –

VIRGO AND ARIES
Subtle, refined Virgos may feel that fiery and volatile Ariens lack tact and finesse. You will bring a dash of practicality and common sense to Ariens, while they will lighten your outlook on life.

Lavender is a Geminian flower

Thistles are ruled by Aries

VIRGO AND GEMINI
Both signs are ruled by Mercury; therefore, you will have no difficulty in communicating. However, a flighty Geminian may not be able to provide you with the stability that you need.

VIRGO AND TAURUS
This is a sensual and well-grounded combination of two steady earth signs. You are both reliable and dependable, and will be able to form a steady, secure, and harmonious partnership.

The lily, and other white flowers, are ruled by Cancer

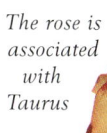

The rose is associated with Taurus

VIRGO AND CANCER
Cancerians are more emotional and sentimental than practical Virgos. However, you have much in common – you are both real worriers, and must keep this trait under control.

– YOU & YOUR LOVER –

VIRGO AND LEO
You have no sympathy for leonine dramatics, but will be attracted by Leo's innate warmth and honesty. This combination should lead to an extremely happy and long-lasting alliance.

Hydrangeas are governed by Libra

Sunflowers are ruled by Leo

VIRGO AND LIBRA
Libra and Virgo make a tactful, kind, and harmonious couple. Librans are calm and easygoing. They will teach you to relax without feeling guilty, and to take life a little less seriously.

VIRGO AND VIRGO
Although you have much in common, this combination may emphasize the Virgoan tendency to worry and criticize. You may be happier with someone who can counteract these traits.

Honeysuckle is attributed to Scorpio

Small, brightly colored flowers are associated with Virgo

VIRGO AND SCORPIO
This is a difficult combination. You have little common ground, but if you can cope with the potent sexuality of Scorpio and do not provoke jealousy, this could be an exciting alliance.

– YOU & YOUR LOVER –

VIRGO AND SAGITTARIUS
This has the potential to be a very happy, successful match. Sagittarian optimism will be quite irresistible to you, and your partner will be attracted by your practicality and honesty.

Orchids are associated with Aquarius

Carnations are ruled by Sagittarius

VIRGO AND AQUARIUS
A self-sufficient Virgo will not threaten the Aquarian need for independence, and this could be a harmonious and long-lasing combination. However, Aquarian eccentricity may irritate you.

VIRGO AND CAPRICORN
Virgo and Capricorn have much in common. You are both honest, practical, and hardworking earth signs. This will be a happy and long-lasting alliance, but you must remember to have a little fun.

Viburnum is governed by Pisces

Pansies are Capricorn flowers

VIRGO AND PISCES
This is the classic attraction of opposites. Your practicality will offset the emotion and romance of Pisces, and the two of you should enjoy a contented and perfectly balanced alliance.

THE FOOD OF LOVE

WHEN PLANNING A SEDUCTION, THE SENSUOUS DELIGHTS OF AN EXQUISITE MEAL SHOULD NEVER BE UNDERESTIMATED. READ ON TO DISCOVER THE PERFECT MEAL FOR EACH OF THE SUN SIGNS, GUARANTEED TO AROUSE INTEREST AND STIR DESIRE.

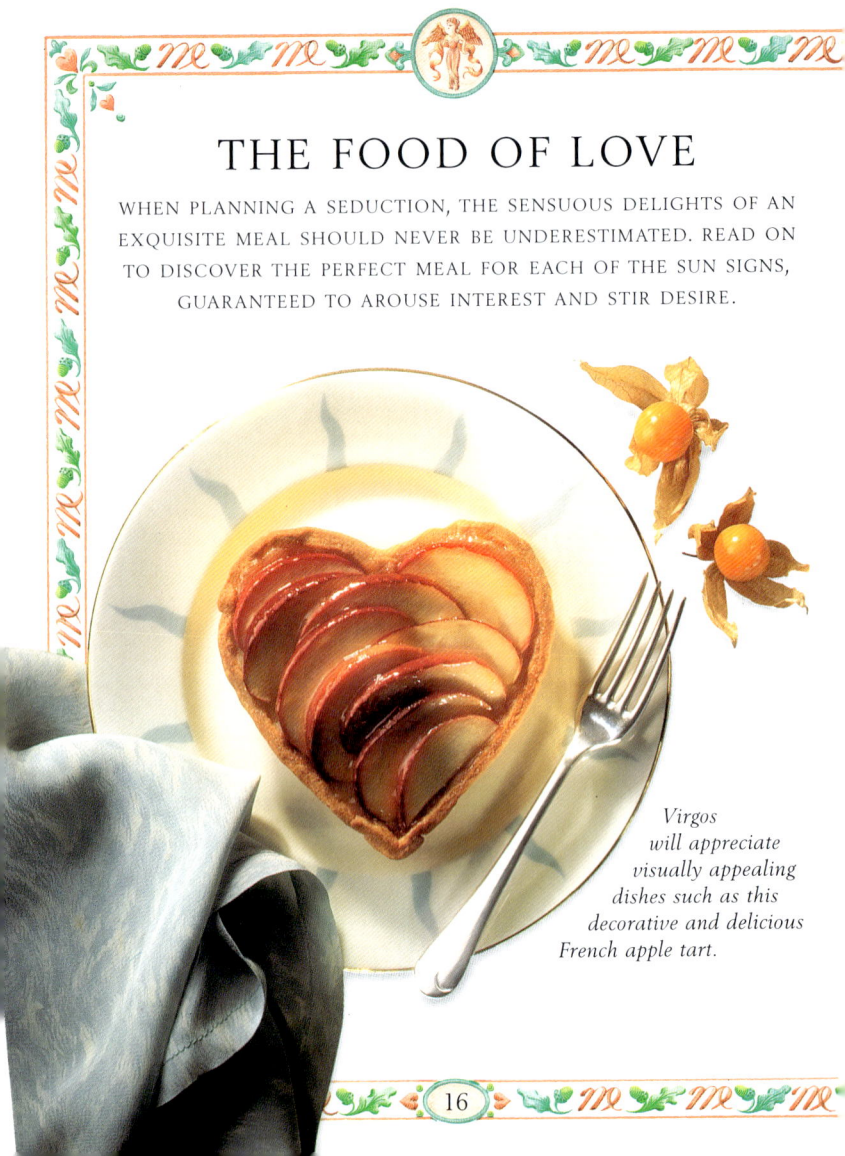

Virgos will appreciate visually appealing dishes such as this decorative and delicious French apple tart.

– THE FOOD OF LOVE –

FOR ARIENS
Spicy mulligatawny soup
·
Peppered steak
·
Baked Alaska

FOR TAUREANS
Cream of cauliflower soup
·
Tournedos Rossini
·
Rich chocolate and brandy mousse

FOR GEMINIANS
Seafood and avocado salad
·
Piquant stir-fried pork with ginger
·
Zabaglione

FOR CANCERIANS
Artichoke vinaigrette
·
Sole Bonne Femme
·
Almond soufflé

– THE FOOD OF LOVE –

FOR LEOS
Roasted tomato and garlic soup
·
Boeuf Stroganoff
·
Pears cooked in wine

FOR VIRGOS
Eggplant salad
·
Paella
·
French apple tart

FOR LIBRANS
Asparagus with hollandaise sauce
·
Pork with roasted apples
·
Strawberry Pavlova

FOR SCORPIOS
Vichyssoise
·
Lobster Newburg
·
Blueberry cream

– THE FOOD OF LOVE –

FOR SAGITTARIANS
Chilled cucumber soup
·
Nutty onion flan
·
Rhubarb crumble with fresh cream

FOR CAPRICORNS
Eggs Florentine
·
Pork tenderloin stuffed with sage
·
Pineapple Pavlova

FOR AQUARIANS
Watercress soup
·
Chicken cooked with chili and lime
·
Lemon soufflé

FOR PISCEANS
French onion soup
·
Trout au vin rosé
·
Melon sorbet

PLACES TO LOVE

ONCE YOU HAVE WON YOUR LOVER'S HEART, A ROMANTIC VACATION TOGETHER WILL SEAL YOUR LOVE. HERE, YOU CAN DISCOVER THE PERFECT DESTINATION FOR EACH SUN SIGN, FROM HISTORIC CITIES TO IDYLLIC BEACHES.

THE EIFFEL TOWER, PARIS

ARIES
Florence is an Arien city, and its perfectly preserved Renaissance palaces and churches will set the scene for wonderful romance.

TAURUS
The unspoiled scenery and unhurried pace of life in rural Ireland is sure to appeal to patient and placid Taureans.

GEMINI
Vivacious and restless Geminians will feel at home in the fast-paced and sophisticated atmosphere of New York.

CANCER
The watery beauty and uniquely romantic atmosphere of Venice is guaranteed to arouse passion and stir the Cancerian imagination.

ST. BASIL'S CATHEDRAL, MOSCOW

AYERS ROCK/ULURU, AUSTRALIA

LEO
Leos will fall in love all over again when surrounded by the picturesque charm and unspoiled medieval atmosphere of Prague.

VIRGO
Perhaps the most elegant and romantic of all cities, Paris is certainly the ideal setting for a stylish and fastidious Virgo.

LIBRA
The dramatic and exotic beauty of Upper Egypt and the Nile will provide the perfect backdrop for wooing a romantic Libran.

SCORPIO
Intense and passionate Scorpios will be strongly attracted by the whiff of danger present in the exotic atmosphere of New Orleans.

SAGITTARIUS
The wide-ranging spaces of the Australian outback will appeal to the Sagittarian love of freedom and the great outdoors.

CAPRICORN
Capricorns will be fascinated and inspired by the great historical monuments of Moscow, the most powerful of all Russian cities.

AQUARIUS
Intrepid Aquarians will be enthralled and amazed by the unusual sights and spectacular landscapes of the Indian subcontinent.

PISCES
Water-loving Pisceans will be at their most relaxed and romantic by the sea, perhaps on a small and unspoiled Mediterranean island.

THE PYRAMIDS, EGYPT

GONDOLAS, VENICE

THE TAJ MAHAL, INDIA

VENUS & MARS

LUCID, SHINING VENUS AND FIERY, RED MARS HAVE ALWAYS BEEN ASSOCIATED WITH HUMAN LOVE AND PASSION. THE TWO PLANETS HAVE A POWERFUL INFLUENCE ON OUR ATTITUDES TOWARD LOVE, SEX, AND RELATIONSHIPS.

The study of astrology first began long before humankind began to record its own history. The earliest astrological artifacts discovered, scratches on bones recording the phases of the Moon, date from well before the invention of any alphabet or writing system.

The planets Venus and Mars have always been regarded as having enormous significance in astrology. This is evident from the tentative attempts of early astrologers to record the effects of the two planets on humankind. Hundreds of years later, the positions of the planets were carefully noted in personal horoscopes. The earliest known record is dated 410 BC: "Venus [was] in the Bull, and Mars in the Twins."

The bright, shining planet Venus represents the gentle effect of the soul on our physical lives. It is responsible for a refined and romantic sensuality – "pure" love, untainted by sex. Venus reigns over our attitudes toward romance and the spiritual dimension of love.

The planet Mars affects the physical aspects of our lives – our strength, both physical and mental; our endurance; and our ability to fight for survival. Mars is also strongly linked to the sex drive of both men and women. Mars governs our physical energy, sexuality, and levels of desire.

Venus is known as an "inferior" planet, because its orbit falls between Earth and the Sun. Venus orbits the Sun

LOVE CONQUERS ALL
In Botticelli's Venus and Mars, *the warlike, fiery energy of Mars, the god of war, has been overcome by the gentle charms of Venus, the goddess of love.*

closely, and its position in the zodiac is always in a sign near that of the Sun. As a result, the planet can only have occupied one of five given signs at the time of your birth – your Sun sign, or the two signs before or after it. For example, if you were born with the Sun in Virgo, Venus can only have occupied Cancer, Leo, Virgo, Libra, or Scorpio at that moment.

Mars, on the other hand, is a "superior" planet. Its orbit lies on the other side of Earth from the Sun, and therefore the planet may have occupied any of the 12 signs at the moment of your birth.

On the following pages (24–45) we provide you with fascinating insights into how Mars and Venus govern your attitudes toward love, sex, and relationships. To ascertain which sign of the zodiac the planets occupied at the moment of your birth, you must first consult the tables on pages 52–61. Then turn to page 24 and read on.

YOUR LOVE LIFE

THE PLANET VENUS REPRESENTS LOVE, HARMONY, AND UNITY. WORK OUT WHICH SIGN OF THE ZODIAC VENUS OCCUPIED AT THE MOMENT OF YOUR BIRTH (SEE PAGES 52–57), AND READ ON.

VENUS IN CANCER

Venus in Cancer will encourage the caring and compassionate qualities of Virgo, and you are likely to gain much satisfaction from looking after people and ensuring that your loved ones are happy and secure.

Your kindness and your ability to tune in to your lover's needs and emotions will prove a great advantage in a permanent relationship. However, try not to allow your loving care for your partner to develop into excessive worry. Cancerians and Virgos are the natural worriers of the zodiac, and you may have to battle against anxiety.

Virgos often have a natural shyness and modesty, which can give them an air of reserve. As a result, they can appear rather cool and detached. From Cancer, Venus will be able to to modify this characteristic, making you warmer and more approachable.

Due to your Virgoan shyness, you may find it difficult to react naturally and spontaneously to your lover's suggestions. This tendency may also be increased by the natural caution of Cancer. You will be so eager to please your partner that you may make the response you think is wanted, rather than giving your honest opinion. Your lover will initially find your eagerness to please flattering, but it could become irritating. Eventually you may become tired of always concurring with your lover's opinions, but by that time it may be too late to change the habit.

- YOUR LOVE LIFE -

Virgo is a very critical sign, and from Cancer Venus will not repress this trait. Why do you criticize your partner? Is it because this person is genuinely at fault, or because you are such a perfectionist that your judgments are too harsh? Try to understand that constant carping and disapproval is hard to bear, and that your criticisms could drive a serious wedge between you and your lover.

Virgos have high standards of cleanliness and tidiness. Do not allow yourself to become neurotic about waging a constant war against mess and dirt.

You are a loyal, supportive, and reliable friend, and will be very popular. However, if you are always refusing invitations on the grounds that you have to clean the bathroom or defrost the freezer, you may end up with no social life at all.

– YOUR LOVE LIFE –

VENUS IN LEO

Traditionally, Virgos have a reputation for being repressed and inhibited, but this image is something of a myth. However, it is true that many Virgos possess elements of shyness and timidity in their personality. Luckily, from Leo, Venus will help to boost your self-confidence and make you less bashful and reserved.

A part of you will always be attracted to glamorous and exciting personalities, but you may find it hard to make the first move toward someone who seems livelier and more extroverted than you. Draw courage from spirited and exuberant Leo, and do not allow any Virgoan shyness and modesty to hold you back.

Venus in Leo will bring you passionate instincts, and these should help to overpower your natural modesty. Give these impulses full rein; increased ardor and desire will benefit both you and your partner. Your Virgoan modesty, spiced with leonine warmth, can make you an irresistible lover.

Your organizational skills are impressive, and will be coupled with plenty of imaginative ideas. You will make a vivacious and lively partner, forever creating enjoyable occasions and events for your lover and friends to participate in. The influence of Leo could make you rather extravagant. You will greatly enjoy spending money, although you may suffer a few Virgoan pangs of guilt when you open your wallet. Try to enjoy the occasional extravagance without feeling too apologetic about it.

Although a Sun-sign Virgo with Venus in Leo will usually find the influence of the fire sign beneficial, this placing of Venus can occasionally give rise to some difficulties. The typical

– YOUR LOVE LIFE –

Virgoan shyness and diffidence and the more dramatic and extroverted qualities of Venus in Leo do not always coexist harmoniously. When you become overexcited, you can behave in an uncharacteristically loud way, only to blush with embarrassment at the thought of what you have just said and done. In time, you will gain the confidence to speak up for yourself without going too far.

This placing of Venus will add a welcome dose of warmth and color to your expression of love and to your personality. Do not try to tone down any leonine exuberance or enthusiasm that manifests itself in your attitude to life. Instead, allow yourself to be as forthcoming and spirited as your nature permits, and you will soon discover that very few people will be able to resist your natural charm for long.

– YOUR LOVE LIFE –

VENUS IN VIRGO

The natural modesty of Virgo will be increased when both Venus and the Sun are in Virgo, and this quality often proves particularly charming and enticing to prospective partners.

However, due to your innate modesty, you may be lacking in self-confidence when it comes to forging relationships. Do not hold back from approaching people you are attracted to because you feel that you are not interesting or attractive enough yourself. Your shyness may prevent you from responding warmly to an approach that you secretly welcome. Try to accept compliments graciously. When these compliments seem to be leading toward more intimate developments, do not let shyness conceal your true feelings.

If problems arise in your relationship, you will not find it difficult to talk them through and resolve them. Virgo is ruled by Mercury, the planet of communication, and as a result those born under this Sun sign tend to be extremely articulate. Once involved in a serious relationship, you should have no difficulty in communicating with your partner and explaining your feelings and opinions. Your natural Virgoan inclination to worry may make you feel agitated about your lover, and suffer extreme concern on his or her behalf. Try to control your tendency toward anxiety by enlisting the help of your down-to-earth outlook on life.

Virgo is a very discriminating and discerning sign, and you are likely to be a perfectionist. As a result, you may develop a tendency to criticize your partner if he or she does not behave exactly to your liking. This need not necessarily be a negative quality, provided your criticisms are constructive and

- YOUR LOVE LIFE -

tactfully worded. However, do not get into the habit of carping and complaining, because this can be fatal to any partnership. Your lover will be worn down by constant criticism, and may even become insecure and lacking in confidence. In addition, you will dislike yourself for constantly denigrating your partner.

Virgo is often portrayed as a repressed and neurotic sign, but many supposedly negative Virgoan characteristics are positive in reality. Your critical streak stems from a tireless search for perfection, your genuine modesty is much more appealing than showiness and vanity, and your tendency to be anxious about your partner is due to your fondness for him or her. Try to present your qualities in a positive light, because you are among the most loyal, devoted, and supportive partners.

– YOUR LOVE LIFE –

VENUS IN LIBRA

The effect of Venus in Libra is a particularly benevolent one. It will help those Virgos who are a little shy and lacking in self-confidence to overcome these weaknesses. You will possess an abundance of natural charm, diplomacy, and tact, and these delightful qualities will greatly increase your powers of attraction.

You have a naturally sympathetic personality, and will be prepared to spend hours listening to and empathizing with the problems of others. This unselfish and helpful trait is guaranteed to endear you to any prospective partners.

Due to the influence of Libra you will feel a strong need to form an emotional relationship. You may not feel completely content and fulfilled until you find a partner, and you may find it hard to realize your full potential when you are single. Although you usually err on the side of caution, you may be very impetuous when it comes to initiating relationships. Do not throw yourself into an affair without pausing to consider how compatible you are. You will be devastated if your relationship goes wrong, and a little thought may prevent much heartache.

The kindhearted and gentle influence of Venus in Libra will soften the critical attitude that so many Virgos possess. Virgo has a reputation for being the most critical of all the Sun signs, perhaps due to the fact that people born under this sign are such perfectionists. Fortunately, your critical faculty will be moderated by this placing of Venus, and you will express any disapproval gently and tactfully. The languid influence of Libra should also calm the Virgoan tendency to worry.

– YOUR LOVE LIFE –

Indecision is one of the few negative traits that Venus can bring from Libra. Virgos often become bogged down in detail and worry about whether they are making the right choices. As a result, they tend to procrastinate and put off making decisions. Venus in Libra may exacerbate this problem, and decision making may always prove to be a struggle. Subconsciously, you may believe that if you vacillate for long enough, your partner will eventually be forced to make a decision for you. Try not to allow this weakness to undermine your admirable practical and analytical qualities.

The marriage of Libran charm and diplomacy with Virgoan supportiveness and modesty will make you a thoughtful and considerate partner. Whoever finally claims you as their own will be very fortunate indeed.

– YOUR LOVE LIFE –

VENUS IN SCORPIO

When Venus shines from Scorpio, the planet will imbue you with an air of sexual and emotional passion that is irresistibly attractive. These qualities can be very seductive, but only if your Virgoan modesty does not suppress them.

Sun-sign Virgos may be intimidated by the powerful influence of Scorpio, because the energy and dynamism of the sign may clash with the retiring disposition of Virgo. Do not try to conceal your passionate personality or play down your attractiveness in order to avoid attention and admiration. Instead of running away from your admirers, concentrate on developing your self-confidence and making the most of yourself.

When you become involved in a sexual relationship, you may find that your Virgoan modesty conflicts with the overt sexuality of Scorpio. Try to relax and savor the pleasures of love without suffering any nagging feelings of guilt and inhibition. Some Virgos have a very chaste and puritanical streak, and feel guilty if they experience too much enjoyment and gratification. However, you need a satisfying and harmonious love life, with both romance and sexuality fully expressed.

The combination of a Virgo Sun sign and Venus in Scorpio will make you a wholehearted and intensely loyal friend. You will go forth into battle on your friends' behalf and will staunchly defend them. In addition, you are a good and sympathetic listener, and will always offer sensible and objective advice. You may find that your friends instinctively turn to you when they are in trouble, and your shoulder may become a little damp from all the tears shed upon on it.

– YOUR LOVE LIFE –

Although you are sympathetic and supportive toward your friends and lovers, you can also be very critical of them. If you must criticize, try to do so in the most diplomatic and constructive manner possible.

The powerful emotions of Scorpio can sometimes be channeled into jealousy and possessiveness. These are not typically Virgoan qualities, but you tend to worry too much, and jealousy and anxiety can be a fatal combination. Use your sensible and practical Virgoan qualities to analyze any pangs of jealousy; you will soon dispose of them once you realize that they are irrational.

If you can combine the plentiful emotion and energy of Scorpio with your Virgoan modesty and intelligence, you will be a loyal, passionate, and supportive friend and lover.

YOUR SEX LIFE

THE PLANET MARS REPRESENTS PHYSICAL AND SEXUAL ENERGY.
WORK OUT WHICH SIGN OF THE ZODIAC MARS OCCUPIED AT THE
MOMENT OF YOUR BIRTH (SEE PAGES 58–61), AND READ ON.

MARS IN ARIES

The vigorous energy and assertiveness of Mars in Aries is guaranteed to invigorate your sexuality.

Virgos can possess a very modest and puritanical attitude toward sex, but the passionate and fiery influence of Aries will undoubtedly prove beneficial in this area. It should overcome any tendency to repress the sensual side of your nature and will give your sex drive a boost.

Virgos are diligent and thorough workers, but can lack ambition and drive. Mars in Aries will increase your energy and determination to succeed. As a result, you will be an exuberant and stimulating partner.

– YOUR SEX LIFE –

MARS IN TAURUS

From Taurus, Mars will boost your sex drive, and will add sensuality and affection to your lovemaking. The ardent and passionate Taurean influence should overcome any Virgoan modesty and shyness when it comes to sexual relationships.

Taurus likes routine and regularity, but you must not allow yourself to become stuck in a rut, always making love at the same time on the same day. Try to be more spontaneous; adhering to a strict routine is not very sexy.

There is a danger that this placing of Mars may encourage you to be possessive. This is not a typical Virgoan characteristic, although you do have a tendency to worry more than is necessary about your lover.

Virgos are generally self-controlled and even-tempered. However, Mars may bring you a hot temper. Once your adrenaline is flowing, you can fly into a sudden rage. Try to calm your temper – dramatic displays of fury may alarm your partner.

– YOUR SEX LIFE –

MARS IN GEMINI

When Mars shines from Gemini the planet will lighten your attitude to love, and you will be an entertaining and imaginative lover.

Virgos can be rather serious-minded about relationships. However, due to the influence of Gemini, you will possess a delightfully flirtatious streak and will revel in the games of courtship and seduction. When it comes to sex, you will be more adventurous and less inhibited than many Virgos.

Very uncharacteristically for a Virgo, the prospect of illicit affairs may appeal to you. However, you will be eager to form a long-term relationship. Apart from any moral considerations, a fear of splitting up will probably persuade you to be faithful to your partner.

Due to the influence of Mars from Gemini, physical attraction alone will not sustain your relationship. An intellectual rapport with your partner will always be equally important.

– YOUR SEX LIFE –

MARS IN CANCER

Due to the influence of Mars from Cancer, you will be more tenderhearted and sentimental than most Virgos. You will long to focus your nurturing instincts on a long-term partner within the confines of a permanent relationship.

Mars in Cancer is a sexually passionate placing, and you and your lover will enjoy an active and sensual sex life. You will be completely faithful to your partners, and will expect total fidelity from them in return.

You have an intuitive awareness of your partner's needs, and will be a generous and caring lover.

If your Virgoan critical streak combines with the energy of Mars in Cancer, you may find that you possess an acid tongue. In moments of anger you can be cruel, not because you are spiteful, but because you cannot resist pointing out to your lover where he or she has gone wrong. Do not allow yourself to become so critical that you destroy your lover's confidence.

– YOUR SEX LIFE –

MARS IN LEO

Those born with Mars in Leo will have a healthy and uncomplicated sexual appetite. Sex will be one of your greatest pleasures, and you will be a skillful and passionate lover. Luxury and comfort are very important to you, and you will seduce your lover in the most plush and elegant surroundings.

This placing will bring good organizational skills and excellent leadership qualities. However, do not become overassertive or domineering toward your lover.

When Mars is in Leo, you will be forthright and outspoken, and may express your Virgoan criticisms more strongly than is necessary. Try not to damage your lover's self-confidence during your outbursts. You like attention, and can occasionally behave in a rather theatrical and ostentatious manner. Try also to resist the temptation to show off, because when your natural Virgoan modesty reasserts itself, you will cringe with embarrassment at the memory.

– YOUR SEX LIFE –

MARS IN VIRGO

When both Mars and the Sun occupy Virgo, you will be a sensitive and self-possessed lover. Your sex drive is moderate, but you can be very sensual and loving when you find the right partner.

You will be eager to form a happy and secure relationship, but the influence of Virgo may make you shy and inhibit the expression of your sexuality. Although you may try to persuade yourself that regular sex is not important to you, an active sex life will benefit you considerably by helping you work out stress or tension. Do not repress your earthy Virgoan sexuality – instead, try to enjoy it.

Virgo is a very discriminating sign, and Mars will make you even more discerning. Try not to be overly critical of your partner, because he or she may begin to resent your disapproving attitude. Virgos tend to be perfectionists, but it is unrealistic to expect everyone to live up to your extremely high standards.

– YOUR SEX LIFE –

MARS IN LIBRA

The energy of Mars can be undermined by the gentle influence of Libra; as a result you may be rather lazy and languid. When Mars shines from Libra, the very prospect of sexual activity may seem exhausting. Fortunately your stores of Virgoan energy should combat any Libran lethargy, and you will be a passionate and exciting lover when aroused.

The influence of Libra is a truly romantic one, and you may fall in love with the very idea of being in love. Virgos can be a little too cool and practical, and a dash of fanciful romance will benefit you greatly. In fact, the gentler qualities that Mars in Libra brings to your personality should help you to relax and lessen your propensity for criticism and complaint.

The peaceable and placid influence of Libra should subdue any innate Virgoan tendency to be critical and deprecating, and you will be a supportive and encouraging lover.

– YOUR SEX LIFE –

MARS IN SCORPIO

The combination of Mars in Scorpio and the Sun in Virgo can be explosive. The passionate and highly sexual influence of Mars in Scorpio will conflict with Virgoan sexual shyness and modesty.

From this sign more than any other, Mars will boost your sexuality. The combination of Scorpio sexual energy and vivacity reined in by Virgoan modesty will be absolutely irresistible. Even if your attitude toward sex is chaste and puritanical, once you are aroused the sexual energy of Scorpio will soon overpower your Virgoan self-control. You must realize that rewarding and satisfying sexual expression is essential for you. If you try to suppress the powerful influence of Mars, you will just become frustrated and dissatisfied.

Overall, there is wonderful potential in this combination. Provided your sexual passions are positively expressed, no lover of yours will ever have cause for complaint.

– YOUR SEX LIFE –

MARS IN SAGITTARIUS

When Mars shines from Sagittarius, it will give an enormous boost to your physical energy. For Virgos, this will be an entirely benevolent influence, particularly because it will allow you to take increased pleasure in the sensual side of love.

There is an element of duality and restlessness in Sagittarius that may tempt you toward infidelity. However, due to your natural Virgoan modesty and self-control, you are unlikely to become involved in illicit liaisons.

You are very lively, and tend to become easily bored. You may abandon what you are doing and rush on to something new, only to repeat the cycle when the novelty has worn off. This tendency may also extend to your relationships. Try not to become involved in a new affair before you have extricated yourself from past entanglements.

Virgos can be critical, and Mars in Sagittarius may make you very blunt. Try to be tactful, and do not become too outspoken.

– YOUR SEX LIFE –

MARS IN CAPRICORN

When Mars shines from Capricorn, you will possess plenty of stamina and will be a skilled and ardent lover with a relaxed and confident attitude toward sex.

You are likely to have an ambitious and competitive edge to your personality, and may be quite ruthless when pursuing a prospective partner. This person will be flattered and intrigued by your determination to win him or her, and will swiftly succumb to your desires.

When wooing a potential partner, you will employ a battery of charms, wining and dining and lavishing the object of your desire with time and attention. However, once you have secured your lover's heart, he or she may have to play second fiddle to your work and your ambitions.

The dangers in such an attitude are obvious. To achieve a happy and fulfilling personal relationship, you must be prepared to sacrifice your worldly ambitions to love.

– YOUR SEX LIFE –

MARS IN AQUARIUS

When Mars shines from Aquarius, you are likely to enjoy an active and exciting sex life once you have overcome your innate Virgoan modesty. Experimentation will play an major role in your lovemaking. You will be prepared to work very hard to ensure that your partner enjoys sexual stimulation and fulfillment.

Your individuality will be emphasized by Mars in Aquarius, and as a result you will be an entertaining and unpredictable lover. The Virgoan passion for neatness and precision will be replaced by a more quirky and unconventional outlook.

From Aquarius, Mars may emphasize a need for freedom and independence, but due to the influence of Virgo, these desires should not trouble you. You require a sense of security and permanence in your sexual relationships, and a brief, flighty affair will be unsatisfactory. Once committed, you are an extremely loyal partner.

– YOUR SEX LIFE –

MARS IN PISCES

The influence of Mars from Pisces will make you a sensual and passionate lover, and should raise your emotional level markedly. With this placing, even a reticent Virgo will not find it difficult to respond to the ardor of a more highly sexual partner.

You are a great romantic and will make great sacrifices and dramatic gestures in the name of love. Your attitude toward relationships is idealistic, and you will expect to experience a true union of body and soul; emotional and physical love are always closely entwined for you.

Fortunately, the sensible and rational Virgoan influence will temper any emotional excesses, and should protect you from suffering heartache if your relationships do not live up to your expectations. If you can balance your Virgoan modesty and practicality with the passion and sensuality of Mars in Pisces, you will be a loyal, supportive, and adoring lover.

TOKENS OF LOVE

ASTROLOGY CAN GIVE YOU A FASCINATING INSIGHT INTO YOUR LOVER'S PERSONALITY AND ATTITUDE TOWARD LOVE. IT CAN ALSO PROVIDE YOU WITH SOME INVALUABLE HINTS WHEN YOU WANT TO CHOOSE THE PERFECT GIFT FOR YOUR LOVER.

ARIES

Ariens tend to be very active and body-conscious; therefore, selected sports equipment is sure to be a successful gift. Aromatherapy massage oils are also guaranteed to delight a sensual Arien lover.

SHUTTLECOCKS

AROMATHERAPY MASSAGE OILS

BELGIAN CHOCOLATE "LEAVES"

TAURUS

Taureans value quality above quantity. Handmade chocolates will appeal, as will fine hand-painted porcelain.

LIMOGES PORCELAIN PILLBOX

GEMINI

Geminians love pieces of jewelry, particularly rings and bracelets.

GOLD PADLOCK BRACELET

– TOKENS OF LOVE –

CANCER

The Cancerian connection with water makes a print of a ship or the ocean a perfect gift. Silver objects are also sure to please.

SILVER TRINKET BOX

SUNFLOWER PEN

19TH-CENTURY PRINT OF AN OCEAN SCENE

LEO

Something entirely unique, such as an original painting or a colorful embroidered cushion will thrill any Leo. The sunflower is the Leo flower; therefore, any objects with a sunflower motif are guaranteed to appeal to your Leo lover.

ORIGINAL OIL PAINTING

WILDFLOWER HONEY

CRYSTALLIZED FRUITS

VIRGO

Instead of chocolates, give your health-conscious Virgo lover a jar of wildflower honey or a box of crystallized fruits.

– TOKENS OF LOVE –

LIBRA
Librans are true romantics and will be delighted by a recording of their favorite classical piece or a video of a sentimental love story.

VIOLIN

CLASSIC FILM POSTER

TABLE LAMP

SCORPIO
A handsome table lamp will be proudly displayed in a Scorpio home. Exotic bath oils will also thrill a sexy Scorpio because Scorpio is a water sign.

SCENTED BATH OIL

ENAMELED GLOBE PILL BOX

SAGITTARIUS
Adventurous, independent Sagittarians love to travel; therefore, any objects with a travel-related theme will be greatly appreciated.

– TOKENS OF LOVE –

OLD-FASHIONED WAXED COTTON UMBRELLA

CANDLES

GLASS DECANTER

CAPRICORN

A traditional umbrella, a heavy glass decanter, or a pair of elegant candles are guaranteed to beguile a fastidious Capricorn lover.

AQUARIUS

Aquarians adore unusual and original presents, such as handmade modern pottery or glass.

HAND-THROWN MODERN POTTERY MUG

ITALIAN CLOWN MASK

GIVING A BIRTHSTONE

The most personal gift you can give your lover is the gem linked to his or her Sun sign.

SARDONYX

ARIES: *diamond*
TAURUS: *emerald*
GEMINI: *agate* • CANCER: *pearl*
LEO: *ruby* • VIRGO: *sardonyx*
LIBRA: *sapphire* • SCORPIO: *opal*
SAGITTARIUS: *topaz*
CAPRICORN: *amethyst*
AQUARIUS: *aquamarine*
PISCES: *moonstone*

PISCES

Secretive, shy Pisceans will be delighted by the gift of an ornamental mask.

YOUR PERMANENT RELATIONSHIP

VIRGOAN CAUTION CAN MAKE YOU HESITANT ABOUT COMMITMENT. HOWEVER, ONCE YOU FEEL SECURE WITHIN A RELATIONSHIP, YOUR CONFIDENCE AND OPTIMISM WILL BLOSSOM.

The morning after you have made a commitment to another person, you will wake up with a sense of apprehensive curiosity and trepidation. However, these emotions will be mingled with a warm and welcome feeling of security.

Virgos tend to be worriers; therefore, you must make a conscious effort to relax into a partnership and to keep your feelings of apprehension under control. You are likely to become overly concerned about even the slightest disruption to your daily routine.

Perfectionism is a typical Virgoan trait, and can cause problems both at home and at work. Your partner may not always understand your conscientious attitude and may find it irritating. If you work, it may be difficult for you to keep your home as spotlessly clean and neat as you would wish. Bear in mind that a slight mess is not the end of the world, and try not to spend so much of your valuable spare time straightening up and cleaning that your lover feels neglected.

Virgos are likely to see themselves as the financial mainstay of the household, even if both partners are working. Therefore, the warning about spending too much time on home chores also applies to the office. You will be a highly conscientious worker, but do not allow this to make you so neurotic and preoccupied about

A JOINT FUTURE
On a Sailing Ship, *by Caspar David Friedrich, shows a newly married couple sailing into a bright but unknown future together.*

your work that you neglect your home and family.

Virgo is reputed to be the least sexual of all the Sun signs, and Virgos are said to be unable to relax into a happy sex life. Happily, this is a total myth, although you may have your fair share of inhibitions. This may be due to the fact that Virgos often underestimate their powers of attraction, and feel insecure about their ability to attract partners. Have more confidence in yourself – do not suppose that your partner makes love to you only out of kindness.

If you can boost your confidence and ignore that nagging voice of worry in your head, you will enjoy a happy and rewarding relationship. Virgoan modesty is charming, but do not allow it to stop you from fully expressing your sexuality.

VENUS & MARS TABLES

THESE TABLES WILL ENABLE YOU TO DISCOVER WHICH SIGNS
VENUS AND MARS OCCUPIED AT THE MOMENT OF YOUR BIRTH.
TURN TO PAGES 24–45 TO INVESTIGATE THE QUALITIES OF THESE
SIGNS, AND TO FIND OUT HOW THEY WORK WITH YOUR SUN SIGN.

The tables on pages 53–61 will enable you to discover the positions of Venus and Mars at the moment of your birth.

First find your year of birth on the top line of the appropriate table, then find your month of birth in the left-hand column. Where the column for your year of birth intersects with the row for your month of birth, you will find a group of figures and zodiacal glyphs. These figures and glyphs show which sign of the zodiac the planet occupied on the first day of that month, and any date during that month on which the planet moved into another sign.

For example, to ascertain the position of Venus on May 10, 1968, run your finger down the column marked 1968 until you reach the row for May. The row of numbers and glyphs shows that Venus occupied Aries on May 1, entered Taurus on May 4, and then moved into Gemini on May 28. Therefore, on May 10, Venus was in Taurus.

If you were born on a day when one of the planets was moving into a new sign, it may be impossible to determine your Venus and Mars signs completely accurately. If the characteristics described on the relevant pages do not seem to apply to you, read the interpretation of the sign before and after. One of these signs will be appropriate.

ZODIACAL GLYPHS

♈	Aries	♎	Libra
♉	Taurus	♏	Scorpio
♊	Gemini	♐	Sagittarius
♋	Cancer	♑	Capricorn
♌	Leo	♒	Aquarius
♍	Virgo	♓	Pisces

– VENUS TABLES –

♀	1921	1922	1923	1924	1925	1926	1927	1928
JAN	1 ♒ / 7 ♓	1 ♑ / 25 ♒	1 ♏ / 13 ♐	1 ♒ / 20 ♓	1 ♐ / 15 ♑	1 ♒	1 ♑ / 10 ♒	1 ♏ / 5 ♐ / 30 ♑
FEB	1 ♓ / 3 ♈	1 ♒ / 18 ♓	1 ♐ / 7 ♑ / 14 ♒	1 ♓ / 14 ♈	1 ♑ / 8 ♒	1 ♒	1 ♒ / 3 ♓ / 27 ♈	1 ♑ / 23 ♒
MAR	1 ♈ / 8 ♉	1 ♓ / 14 ♈	1 ♑ / 7 ♒	1 ♈ / 10 ♉	1 ♒ / 5 ♓ / 29 ♈	1 ♒	1 ♈ / 23 ♉	1 ♒ / 19 ♓
APR	1 ♉ / 26 ♈	1 ♈ / 7 ♉	1 ♒ / 2 ♓ / 27 ♈	1 ♉ / 6 ♈	1 ♈ / 22 ♉	1 ♒ / 7 ♓	1 ♉ / 17 ♊	1 ♓ / 12 ♈
MAY	1 ♈	1 ♉ / 2 ♊ / 26 ♋	1 ♈ / 22 ♉	1 ♊ / 7 ♋	1 ♉ / 16 ♊	1 ♓ / 7 ♈	1 ♊ / 13 ♋	1 ♈ / 7 ♉ / 31 ♊
JUN	1 ♈ / 3 ♉	1 ♋ / 20 ♌	1 ♉ / 16 ♊	1 ♋	1 ♊ / 10 ♋	1 ♈ / 3 ♉ / 29 ♊	1 ♋ / 9 ♌	1 ♊ / 24 ♋
JUL	1 ♉ / 9 ♊	1 ♌ / 16 ♍	1 ♊ / 11 ♋	1 ♋	1 ♋ / 4 ♌ / 29 ♍	1 ♊ / 25 ♋	1 ♌ / 8 ♍	1 ♋ / 19 ♌
AUG	1 ♊ / 6 ♋	1 ♍ / 11 ♎	1 ♋ / 4 ♌ / 28 ♍	1 ♋	1 ♍ / 23 ♎	1 ♋ / 19 ♌	1 ♍	1 ♋ / 12 ♌
SEP	1 ♌ / 27 ♍	1 ♎ / 8 ♏	1 ♍ / 22 ♎	1 ♋ / 8 ♌ / —	1 ♎ / 17 ♏	1 ♌ / 12 ♍	1 ♍	1 ♍ / 5 ♎ / 30 ♏
OCT	1 ♍ / 21 ♎	1 ♏ / 11 ♐	1 ♎ / 16 ♏	1 ♌ / 8 ♍	1 ♏ / 12 ♐	1 ♍ / 6 ♎ / 30 ♏	1 ♍	1 ♏ / 24 ♐
NOV	1 ♎ / 14 ♏	1 ♐ / 29 ♏	1 ♏ / 9 ♐	1 ♍ / 3 ♎ / 28 ♏	1 ♐ / 7 ♑	1 ♏ / 23 ♐	1 ♎ / 10 ♏	1 ♐ / 18 ♑
DEC	1 ♏ / 8 ♐	1 ♏	1 ♐ / 3 ♑ / 27 ♒	1 ♏ / 22 ♐	1 ♑ / 6 ♒	1 ♐ / 17 ♑	1 ♏ / 9 ♐	1 ♑ / 13 ♒

♀	1929	1930	1931	1932	1933	1934	1935	1936
JAN	1 ♒ / 7 ♓	1 ♑ / 25 ♒	1 ♏ / 4 ♐	1 ♒ / 20 ♓	1 ♐ / 15 ♑	1 ♒	1 ♑ / 9 ♒	1 ♏ / 4 ♐ / 29 ♑
FEB	1 ♓ / 3 ♈	1 ♒ / 17 ♓	1 ♐ / 7 ♑	1 ♓ / 13 ♈	1 ♑ / 8 ♒	1 ♒	1 ♒ / 2 ♓ / 27 ♈	1 ♑ / 23 ♒
MAR	1 ♈ / 9 ♉	1 ♓ / 13 ♈	1 ♑ / 6 ♒	1 ♈ / 10 ♉	1 ♒ / 4 ♓ / 28 ♈	1 ♒	1 ♈ / 23 ♉	1 ♒ / 18 ♓
APR	1 ♉ / 21 ♈	1 ♈ / 7 ♉	1 ♒ / 27 ♓	1 ♉ / 6 ♈	1 ♈ / 21 ♉	1 ♒ / 7 ♓	1 ♉ / 17 ♊	1 ♓ / 12 ♈
MAY	1 ♈	1 ♉ / 26 ♊ / ♋	1 ♈ / 22 ♉	1 ♊ / 7 ♋	1 ♉ / 16 ♊	1 ♓ / 7 ♈	1 ♊ / 12 ♋	1 ♈ / 6 ♉ / 30 ♊
JUN	1 ♈ / 4 ♉	1 ♋ / 20 ♌	1 ♉ / 15 ♊	1 ♋	1 ♊ / 9 ♋	1 ♈ / 3 ♉ / 29 ♊	1 ♋ / 8 ♌	1 ♊ / 24 ♋
JUL	1 ♉ / 9 ♊	1 ♌ / 15 ♍	1 ♊ / 10 ♋	1 ♋ / 14 ♊ / 29 ♋	1 ♋ / 4 ♌ / 28 ♍	1 ♊ / 24 ♋	1 ♌ / 8 ♍	1 ♋ / 18 ♌
AUG	1 ♊ / 6 ♋	1 ♍ / 11 ♎	1 ♋ / 4 ♌ / 28 ♍	1 ♋	1 ♍ / 22 ♎	1 ♋ / 18 ♌	1 ♍	1 ♋ / 12 ♌
SEP	1 ♌ / 26 ♍	1 ♎ / 8 ♏	1 ♍ / 21 ♎	1 ♋ / 9 ♌	1 ♎ / 16 ♏	1 ♌ / 12 ♍	1 ♍	1 ♍ / 5 ♎ / 29 ♏
OCT	1 ♍ / 21 ♎	1 ♏ / 13 ♐	1 ♎ / 15 ♏	1 ♌ / 8 ♍	1 ♏ / 12 ♐	1 ♍ / 6 ♎ / 30 ♏	1 ♍	1 ♏ / 24 ♐
NOV	1 ♎ / 14 ♏	1 ♐ / 23 ♏	1 ♏ / 8 ♐	1 ♍ / 3 ♎ / 28 ♏	1 ♐ / 7 ♑	1 ♏ / 23 ♐	1 ♎ / 10 ♏	1 ♐ / 17 ♑
DEC	1 ♏ / 8 ♐ / 31 ♑	1 ♏	1 ♐ / 2 ♑ / 26 ♒	1 ♏ / 22 ♐	1 ♑ / 6 ♒	1 ♐ / 17 ♑	1 ♎ / 9 ♏	1 ♑ / 12 ♒

VENUS TABLES

♀	1937	1938	1939	1940	1941	1942	1943	1944
JAN	1 ♒ 7 ♓	1 ♑ 24 ♒	1 ♏ 5 ♐	1 ♒ 19 ♓	1 ♐ 14 ♑	1 ♒	1 ♑ 9 ♒	1 ♏ 4 ♐ 29 ♑
FEB	1 ♓ 3 ♈	1 ♒ 17 ♓	1 ♐ 7 ♑	1 ♓ 13 ♈	1 ♑ 7 ♒	1 ♒	1 ♒ 2 ♓ 26 ♈	1 ♑ 22 ♒
MAR	1 ♈ 10 ♉	1 ♓ 13 ♈	1 ♑ 6 ♒	1 ♈ 9 ♉	1 ♒ 3 ♓ 28 ♈	1 ♒	1 ♈ 22 ♉	1 ♒ 18 ♓
APR	1 ♉ 15 ♈	1 ♈ 6 ♉ 30 ♊	1 ♓ 26 ♈	1 ♉ 5 ♊	1 ♈ 21 ♉	1 ♒ 7 ♓	1 ♉ 16 ♊	1 ♓ 11 ♈
MAY	1 ♈	1 ♊ 25 ♋	1 ♈ 21 ♉	1 ♊ 15 ♋	1 ♉ 15 ♊	1 ♓ 7 ♈	1 ♊ 12 ♋	1 ♈ 5 ♉ 30 ♊
JUN	1 ♈ 5 ♉	1 ♋ 19 ♌	1 ♉ 15 ♊	1 ♋	1 ♊ 8 ♋	1 ♈ 3 ♉ 28 ♊	1 ♋ 8 ♌	1 ♊ 23 ♋
JUL	1 ♉ 8 ♊	1 ♌ 15 ♍	1 ♊ 10 ♋	1 ♋ 6 ♊	1 ♋ 3 ♌ 28 ♍	1 ♊ 24 ♋	1 ♌ 8 ♍	1 ♋ 18 ♌
AUG	1 ♊ 5 ♋	1 ♍ 10 ♎	1 ♋ 3 ♌ 27 ♍	1 ♊ 2 ♋	1 ♍ 22 ♎	1 ♋ 18 ♌	1 ♍	1 ♌ 11 ♍
SEP	1 ♌ 26 ♍	1 ♎ 8 ♏	1 ♍ 21 ♎	1 ♋ 9 ♌	1 ♎ 16 ♏	1 ♌ 11 ♍	1 ♍	1 ♍ 4 ♎ 29 ♏
OCT	1 ♍ 20 ♎	1 ♏ 14 ♐	1 ♎ 15 ♏	1 ♌ 7 ♍	1 ♏ 11 ♐	1 ♍ 5 ♎ 29 ♏	1 ♍	1 ♏ 23 ♐
NOV	1 ♎ 13 ♏	1 ♐ 16 ♏	1 ♏ 8 ♐	1 ♍ 2 ♎ 27 ♏	1 ♐ 7 ♑	1 ♏ 22 ♐	1 ♍ 10 ♎	1 ♐ 17 ♑
DEC	1 ♏ 7 ♐ 31 ♑	1 ♏	1 ♐ 2 ♑ 26 ♒	1 ♏ 21 ♐	1 ♑ 6 ♒	1 ♐ 16 ♑	1 ♎ 9 ♏	1 ♑ 12 ♒

♀	1945	1946	1947	1948	1949	1950	1951	1952
JAN	1 ♒ 6 ♓	1 ♑ 23 ♒	1 ♏ 6 ♐	1 ♒ 19 ♓	1 ♐ 14 ♑	1 ♒	1 ♑ 8 ♒	1 ♏ 3 ♐ 28 ♑
FEB	1 ♓ 3 ♈	1 ♒ 16 ♓	1 ♐ 7 ♑	1 ♓ 12 ♈	1 ♑ 7 ♒	1 ♒	1 ♓ 25 ♈	1 ♑ 21 ♒
MAR	1 ♈ 12 ♉	1 ♓ 12 ♈	1 ♑ 6 ♒ 31 ♓	1 ♈ 9 ♉	1 ♒ 3 ♓ 27 ♈	1 ♒	1 ♈ 22 ♉	1 ♒ 17 ♓
APR	1 ♉ 8 ♈	1 ♈ 6 ♉ 30 ♊	1 ♓ 26 ♈	1 ♉ 5 ♊	1 ♈ 20 ♉	1 ♒ 7 ♓	1 ♉ 16 ♊	1 ♓ 10 ♈
MAY	1 ♈	1 ♊ 25 ♋	1 ♈ 21 ♉	1 ♉ 8 ♊	1 ♊ 15 ♋	1 ♉ 6 ♊	1 ♓ 6 ♈	1 ♊ 12 ♋	1 ♈ 5 ♉ 29 ♊
JUN	1 ♈ 5 ♉	1 ♋ 19 ♌	1 ♉ 14 ♊	1 ♋ 30 ♊	1 ♊ 8 ♋	1 ♊ 2 ♋ 28 ♌	1 ♋ 8 ♌	1 ♊ 23 ♋
JUL	1 ♉ 8 ♊	1 ♌ 14 ♍	1 ♊ 9 ♋	1 ♊	1 ♋ 2 ♌ 27 ♍	1 ♋ 23 ♌	1 ♌ 8 ♍	1 ♋ 17 ♌
AUG	1 ♊ 5 ♋ 31 ♌	1 ♍ 10 ♎	1 ♋ 3 ♌ 27 ♍	1 ♊ 4 ♋	1 ♍ 21 ♎	1 ♋ 17 ♌	1 ♍	1 ♌ 10 ♍
SEP	1 ♌ 25 ♍	1 ♎ 8 ♏	1 ♍ 20 ♎	1 ♋ 9 ♌	1 ♎ 15 ♏	1 ♌ 11 ♍	1 ♍	1 ♍ 4 ♎ 28 ♏
OCT	1 ♍ 20 ♎	1 ♏ 17 ♐	1 ♎ 14 ♏	1 ♌ 7 ♍	1 ♏ 11 ♐	1 ♍ 5 ♎ 29 ♏	1 ♍	1 ♏ 23 ♐
NOV	1 ♎ 13 ♏	1 ♐ 9 ♏	1 ♏ 7 ♐	1 ♍ 2 ♎ 27 ♏	1 ♐ 7 ♑	1 ♏ 22 ♐	1 ♍ 10 ♎	1 ♐ 16 ♑
DEC	1 ♏ 7 ♐ 31 ♑	1 ♏	1 ♑ 25 ♒	1 ♏ 21 ♐	1 ♑ 7 ♒	1 ♐ 15 ♑	1 ♎ 9 ♏	1 ♑ 11 ♒

– VENUS TABLES –

♀	1953	1954	1955	1956	1957	1958	1959	1960
JAN	1 ♒ 6 ♓	1 ♑ 23 ♒	1 ♏ 7 ♐	1 ♒ 18 ♓	1 ♐ 13 ♑	1 ♒	1 ♑ 8 ♒	1 ♏ 3 ♐ 28 ♑
FEB	1 ♓ 3 ♈	1 ♒ 16 ♓	1 ♐ 7 ♑	1 ♓ 12 ♈	1 ♑ 6 ♒	1 ♒	1 ♒ 25 ♓	1 ♑ 21 ♒
MAR	1 ♈ 15 ♉	1 ♓ 12 ♈	1 ♑ 5 ♒ 31 ♓	1 ♈ 8 ♉	1 ♒ 2 ♓ 26 ♈	1 ♒	1 ♈ 21 ♉	1 ♒ 16 ♓
APR	1 ♈	1 ♉ 5 ♊ 29 ♋	1 ♓ 25 ♈	1 ♉ 5 ♊	1 ♈ 19 ♉	1 ♒ 7 ♓	1 ♉ 15 ♊	1 ♓ 10 ♈
MAY	1 ♈	1 ♊ 24 ♋	1 ♈ 20 ♉	1 ♊ 9 ♋	1 ♉ 14 ♊	1 ♓ 6 ♈	1 ♊ 11 ♋	1 ♈ 4 ♉ 29 ♊
JUN	1 ♈ 6 ♉	1 ♋ 18 ♌	1 ♉ 14 ♊	1 ♋ 24 ♊	1 ♊ 7 ♋	1 ♈ 2 ♉ 27 ♊	1 ♋ 7 ♌	1 ♊ 22 ♋
JUL	1 ♉ 8 ♊	1 ♌ 14 ♍	1 ♊ 9 ♋	1 ♊	1 ♋ 2 ♌ 27 ♍	1 ♊ 22 ♋	1 ♌ 9 ♍	1 ♋ 16 ♌
AUG	1 ♊ 5 ♋ 31 ♌	1 ♍ 10 ♎	1 ♋ 2 ♌ 26 ♍	1 ♊ 5 ♋	1 ♍ 21 ♎	1 ♋ 16 ♌	1 ♍	1 ♌ 9 ♍
SEP	1 ♌ 25 ♍	1 ♎ 7 ♏	1 ♍ 19 ♎	1 ♋ 9 ♌	1 ♎ 15 ♏	1 ♌ 10 ♍	1 ♍ 21 ♎ 26 ♍	1 ♌ 3 ♍ 28 ♏
OCT	1 ♍ 19 ♎	1 ♏ 24 ♐ 28 ♏	1 ♎ 13 ♏	1 ♌ 11 ♍	1 ♏ 3 ♐ 28 ♏	1 ♍	1 ♏ 22 ♐
NOV	1 ♎ 12 ♏	1 ♏	1 ♏ 6 ♐	1 ♍ 26 ♏	1 ♏ 6 ♐	1 ♐ 21 ♑	1 ♏ 6 ♐	1 ♍ 10 ♎	1 ♐ 16 ♑
DEC	1 ♏ 6 ♐ 30 ♑	1 ♏	1 ♑ 25 ♒	1 ♏ 20 ♐	1 ♑ 7 ♒	1 ♐ 15 ♑	1 ♎ 8 ♏	1 ♑ 11 ♒

♀	1961	1962	1963	1964	1965	1966	1967	1968
JAN	1 ♒ 6 ♓	1 ♑ 22 ♒	1 ♏ 7 ♐	1 ♒ 17 ♓	1 ♐ 13 ♑	1 ♒	1 ♑ 7 ♒ 31 ♓	1 ♏ 2 ♐ 27 ♑
FEB	1 ♓ 3 ♈	1 ♒ 15 ♓	1 ♐ 6 ♑	1 ♓ 11 ♈	1 ♑ 6 ♒	1 ♑ 7 ♒ 26 ♓	1 ♓ 24 ♈	1 ♑ 21 ♒
MAR	1 ♈	1 ♓ 11 ♈	1 ♑ 5 ♒ 31 ♓	1 ♈ 8 ♉	1 ♒ 2 ♓ 26 ♈	1 ♒	1 ♈ 21 ♉	1 ♒ 16 ♓
APR	1 ♈	1 ♈ 4 ♉ 29 ♊	1 ♓ 25 ♈	1 ♉ 5 ♊	1 ♈ 19 ♉	1 ♈ 7 ♉	1 ♒ 7 ♓	1 ♉ 15 ♊	1 ♓ 9 ♈
MAY	1 ♈	1 ♊ 24 ♋	1 ♈ 19 ♉	1 ♊ 10 ♋	1 ♉ 13 ♊	1 ♓ 6 ♈	1 ♊ 11 ♋	1 ♈ 4 ♉ 28 ♊
JUN	1 ♈ 6 ♉	1 ♋ 18 ♌	1 ♉ 13 ♊	1 ♋ 18 ♊	1 ♊ 7 ♋	1 ♊ 27 ♋	1 ♋ 8 ♌	1 ♊ 21 ♋
JUL	1 ♉ 8 ♊	1 ♌ 13 ♍	1 ♊ 8 ♋	1 ♊	1 ♋ 26 ♍	1 ♋ 22 ♌	1 ♌ 9 ♍	1 ♋ 16 ♌
AUG	1 ♊ 4 ♋ 30 ♌	1 ♍ 9 ♎	1 ♌ 26 ♍	1 ♊ 6 ♋	1 ♍ 20 ♎	1 ♍ 16 ♎	1 ♍	1 ♌ 9 ♍
SEP	1 ♌ 25 ♍	1 ♎ 8 ♏	1 ♍ 18 ♎	1 ♋ 9 ♌	1 ♎ 14 ♏	1 ♌ 9 ♍	1 ♍ 10 ♎	1 ♍ 3 ♎ 27 ♏
OCT	1 ♍ 18 ♎	1 ♏	1 ♎ 13 ♏	1 ♌ 10 ♍	1 ♏ 3 ♐ 27 ♏	1 ♎ 2 ♍	1 ♏ 22 ♐
NOV	1 ♎ 12 ♏	1 ♏	1 ♏ 6 ♐ 30 ♑	1 ♎ 2 ♏	1 ♏ 6 ♐	1 ♐ 20 ♑	1 ♏ 6 ♐	1 ♍ 15 ♎	1 ♐ 15 ♑
DEC	1 ♏ 6 ♐ 29 ♑	1 ♏	1 ♑ 24 ♒	1 ♏ 20 ♐	1 ♑ 8 ♒	1 ♐ 14 ♑	1 ♎ 8 ♏	1 ♑ 10 ♒

- VENUS TABLES -

♀	1969	1970	1971	1972	1973	1974	1975	1976
JAN	1 5 ♒ ♓	1 22 ♑ ♒	1 8 ♏ ♐	1 17 ♒ ♓	1 12 ♐ ♑	1 30 ♒ ♑	1 7 31 ♑ ♒ ♓	1 2 27 ♏ ♐ ♑
FEB	1 3 ♓ ♈	1 15 ♒ ♓	1 6 ♐ ♑	1 11 ♓ ♈	1 5 ♑ ♒	1 ♑	1 24 ♓ ♈	1 20 ♑ ♒
MAR	1 ♈	1 11 ♓ ♈	1 5 30 ♑ ♒ ♓	1 8 ♈ ♉	1 25 ♓ ♈	1 ♒	1 20 ♈ ♉	1 15 ♒ ♓
APR	1 ♈	1 4 28 ♈ ♉ ♊	1 24 ♓ ♈	1 4 ♉ ♊	1 19 ♈ ♉	1 7 ♒ ♓	1 14 ♉ ♊	1 9 ♓ ♈
MAY	1 ♈	1 23 ♊ ♋	1 19 ♈ ♉	1 11 ♊ ♋	1 13 ♉ ♊	1 5 ♓ ♈	1 10 ♊ ♋	1 3 27 ♈ ♉ ♊
JUN	1 6 ♈ ♉	1 17 ♋ ♌	1 13 ♉ ♊	1 12 ♋ ♊	1 6 ♊ ♋	1 26 ♉ ♊	1 7 ♋ ♌	1 21 ♊ ♋
JUL	1 7 ♉ ♊	1 13 ♌ ♍	1 7 ♊ ♋	1 ♊	1 26 ♋ ♌	1 22 ♊ ♋	1 10 ♌ ♍	1 15 ♋ ♌
AUG	1 4 30 ♊ ♋ ♌	1 9 ♍ ♎	1 25 ♌ ♍	1 7 ♊ ♋	1 19 ♍ ♎	1 15 ♋ ♌	1 ♍	1 9 ♌ ♍
SEP	1 24 ♌ ♍	1 8 ♎ ♏	1 18 ♍ ♎	1 8 ♋ ♌	1 14 ♎ ♏	1 9 ♌ ♍	1 3 ♍ ♎	1 2 26 ♍ ♎ ♏
OCT	1 18 ♍ ♎	1 ♏	1 12 ♎ ♏	1 6 31 ♌ ♍ ♎	1 10 ♏ ♐	1 3 27 ♍ ♎ ♏	1 5 ♎ ♏	1 21 ♏ ♐
NOV	1 11 ♎ ♏	1 ♏	1 5 30 ♏ ♐ ♑	1 25 ♎ ♏	1 6 ♐ ♑	1 20 ♏ ♐	1 10 ♍ ♎	1 15 ♐ ♑
DEC	1 5 29 ♏ ♐ ♑	1 ♏	1 24 ♑ ♒	1 19 ♏ ♐	1 8 ♑ ♒	1 14 ♐ ♑	1 7 ♎ ♏	1 10 ♑ ♒

♀	1977	1978	1979	1980	1981	1982	1983	1984
JAN	1 5 ♒ ♓	1 21 ♑ ♒	1 8 ♏ ♐	1 16 ♒ ♓	1 12 ♐ ♑	1 24 ♒ ♑	1 6 30 ♑ ♒ ♓	1 2 26 ♏ ♐ ♑
FEB	1 3 ♓ ♈	1 14 ♒ ♓	1 6 ♐ ♑	1 10 ♓ ♈	1 5 28 ♑ ♒ ♓	1 ♑	1 23 ♓ ♈	1 20 ♑ ♒
MAR	1 ♈	1 10 ♓ ♈	1 4 29 ♑ ♒ ♓	1 7 ♈ ♉	1 25 ♓ ♈	1 3 ♑ ♒	1 20 ♈ ♉	1 15 ♒ ♓
APR	1 ♈	1 3 28 ♈ ♉ ♊	1 23 ♓ ♈	1 4 ♉ ♊	1 18 ♈ ♉	1 7 ♒ ♓	1 14 ♉ ♊	1 8 ♓ ♈
MAY	1 ♈	1 22 ♊ ♋	1 18 ♈ ♉	1 13 ♊ ♋	1 12 ♉ ♊	1 5 31 ♓ ♈ ♉	1 10 ♊ ♋	1 3 27 ♈ ♉ ♊
JUN	1 7 ♈ ♉	1 17 ♋ ♌	1 12 ♉ ♊	1 6 ♋ ♊	1 6 30 ♊ ♋ ♌	1 26 ♉ ♊	1 7 ♋ ♌	1 21 ♊ ♋
JUL	1 7 ♉ ♊	1 12 ♌ ♍	1 7 31 ♊ ♋ ♌	1 ♊	1 25 ♌ ♍	1 21 ♊ ♋	1 11 ♌ ♍	1 15 ♋ ♌
AUG	1 3 29 ♊ ♋ ♌	1 8 ♍ ♎	1 25 ♌ ♍	1 7 ♊ ♋	1 19 ♍ ♎	1 15 ♋ ♌	1 28 ♍ ♌	1 8 ♌ ♍
SEP	1 23 ♌ ♍	1 8 ♎ ♏	1 18 ♍ ♎	1 8 ♌ ♎	1 13 ♎ ♏	1 8 ♌ ♍	1 ♌	1 2 26 ♍ ♎ ♏
OCT	1 17 ♍ ♎	1 ♏	1 12 ♎ ♏	1 5 31 ♌ ♍ ♎	1 9 ♏ ♐	1 2 26 ♍ ♎ ♏	1 6 ♌ ♍	1 21 ♏ ♐
NOV	1 11 ♎ ♏	1 ♏	1 5 29 ♏ ♐ ♑	1 25 ♎ ♏	1 6 ♐ ♑	1 19 ♏ ♐	1 10 ♍ ♎	1 14 ♐ ♑
DEC	1 4 28 ♏ ♐ ♑	1 ♏	1 23 ♑ ♒	1 19 ♏ ♐	1 9 ♑ ♒	1 12 ♐ ♑	1 7 ♎ ♏	1 10 ♑ ♒

– VENUS TABLES –

♀	1985	1986	1987	1988	1989	1990	1991	1992
JAN	1 ♒ 5 ♓	1 ♑ 21 ♒	1 ♏ 8 ♐	1 ♒ 16 ♓	1 ♐ 7 ♑	1 ♒ 17 ♑	1 ♑ 6 ♒ 30 ♓	1 ♐ 26 ♑
FEB	1 ♓ 3 ♈	1 ♒ 14 ♓	1 ♐ 6 ♑	1 ♓ 10 ♈	1 ♑ 4 ♒ 28 ♓	1 ♑	1 ♓ 23 ♈	1 ♑ 19 ♒
MAR	1 ♈	1 ♓ 9 ♈	1 ♑ 4 ♒ 29 ♓	1 ♈ 7 ♉	1 ♓ 24 ♈	1 ♑ 4 ♒	1 ♈ 19 ♉	1 ♒ 14 ♓
APR	1 ♈	1 ♈ 3 ♉ 27 ♊	1 ♓ 23 ♈	1 ♉ 4 ♊	1 ♈ 17 ♉	1 ♒ 7 ♓	1 ♉ 13 ♊	1 ♓ 7 ♈
MAY	1 ♈	1 ♊ 22 ♋	1 ♈ 18 ♉	1 ♊ 18 ♋ 27 ♊	1 ♉ 12 ♊	1 ♓ 4 ♈ 31 ♉	1 ♊ 9 ♋	1 ♈ 2 ♉ 26 ♊
JUN	1 ♈ 7 ♉	1 ♋ 16 ♌	1 ♉ 12 ♊	1 ♊	1 ♊ 5 ♋ 30 ♌	1 ♉ 25 ♊	1 ♋ 7 ♌	1 ♊ 20 ♋
JUL	1 ♉ 7 ♊	1 ♌ 12 ♍	1 ♊ 6 ♋ 31 ♌	1 ♊	1 ♌ 24 ♍	1 ♊ 20 ♋	1 ♌ 11 ♍	1 ♋ 14 ♌
AUG	1 ♊ 3 ♋ 28 ♌	1 ♍ 8 ♎	1 ♌ 24 ♍	1 ♊ 7 ♋	1 ♍ 18 ♎	1 ♋ 13 ♌	1 ♍ 22 ♎	1 ♌ 17 ♍
SEP	1 ♌ 23 ♍	1 ♎ 8 ♏	1 ♍ 17 ♎	1 ♋ 8 ♌	1 ♎ 13 ♏	1 ♌ 9 ♍	1 ♍	1 ♍ 25 ♎
OCT	1 ♍ 17 ♎	1 ♏	1 ♎ 11 ♏	1 ♌ 5 ♍ 30 ♎	1 ♏ 9 ♐	1 ♍ 2 ♎ 26 ♏	1 ♍ 7 ♎	1 ♎ 7 ♏
NOV	1 ♎ 10 ♏	1 ♏	1 ♏ 4 ♐ 28 ♑	1 ♎ 24 ♏	1 ♐ 6 ♑	1 ♏ 19 ♐	1 ♎ 9 ♏	1 ♏ 14 ♐
DEC	1 ♏ 4 ♐ 28 ♑	1 ♏	1 ♑ 23 ♒	1 ♏ 18 ♐	1 ♑ 10 ♒	1 ♐ 13 ♑	1 ♏ 7 ♐	1 ♑ 9 ♒

♀	1993	1994	1995	1996	1997	1998	1999	2000
JAN	1 ♒ 4 ♓	1 ♑ 20 ♒	1 ♏ 8 ♐	1 ♒ 15 ♓	1 ♐ 7 ♑	1 ♒ 10 ♑	1 ♑ 5 ♒ 29 ♓	1 ♐ 25 ♑
FEB	1 ♓ 3 ♈	1 ♒ 13 ♓	1 ♐ 5 ♑	1 ♓ 9 ♈	1 ♑ 4 ♒ 28 ♓	1 ♑	1 ♓ 22 ♈	1 ♑ 19 ♒
MAR	1 ♈	1 ♓ 9 ♈	1 ♑ 3 ♒ 29 ♓	1 ♈ 6 ♉	1 ♓ 24 ♈	1 ♑ 5 ♒	1 ♈ 19 ♉	1 ♒ 14 ♓
APR	1 ♈	1 ♈ 2 ♉ 27 ♊	1 ♓ 23 ♈	1 ♉ 4 ♊	1 ♈ 17 ♉	1 ♒ 7 ♓	1 ♉ 13 ♊	1 ♓ 7 ♈
MAY	1 ♈	1 ♊ 21 ♋	1 ♈ 17 ♉	1 ♊	1 ♉ 11 ♊	1 ♓ 4 ♈ 30 ♉	1 ♊ 9 ♋	1 ♈ 2 ♉ 26 ♊
JUN	1 ♈ 7 ♉	1 ♋ 15 ♌	1 ♉ 11 ♊	1 ♊	1 ♊ 4 ♋ 29 ♌	1 ♉ 25 ♊	1 ♋ 6 ♌	1 ♊ 19 ♋
JUL	1 ♉ 6 ♊	1 ♌ 12 ♍	1 ♊ 6 ♋ 30 ♌	1 ♊	1 ♌ 24 ♍	1 ♊ 20 ♋	1 ♌ 13 ♍	1 ♋ 14 ♌
AUG	1 ♊ 2 ♋ 28 ♌	1 ♍ 8 ♎	1 ♌ 23 ♍	1 ♊ 8 ♋	1 ♍ 18 ♎	1 ♋ 14 ♌	1 ♍ 16 ♎	1 ♌ 17 ♍
SEP	1 ♌ 22 ♍	1 ♎ 8 ♏	1 ♍ 17 ♎	1 ♋ 8 ♌	1 ♎ 12 ♏	1 ♌ 7 ♍	1 ♍	1 ♍ 25 ♎
OCT	1 ♍ 16 ♎	1 ♏	1 ♎ 11 ♏	1 ♌ 5 ♍ 30 ♎	1 ♏ 9 ♐	1 ♎ 25 ♏	1 ♍ 8 ♎	1 ♎ 20 ♏
NOV	1 ♎ 9 ♏	1 ♏	1 ♏ 4 ♐ 28 ♑	1 ♎ 23 ♏	1 ♐ 6 ♑	1 ♏ 18 ♐	1 ♎ 10 ♏	1 ♐ 13 ♑
DEC	1 ♏ 3 ♐ 27 ♑	1 ♏	1 ♑ 22 ♒	1 ♏ 17 ♐	1 ♑ 12 ♒	1 ♐ 12 ♑	1 ♎ 6 ♏	1 ♑ 9 ♒

MARS TABLES

♂	1921	1922	1923	1924	1925	1926	1927	1928	1929	1930
JAN	1 ♒ 5 ♓	1 ♏	1 ♓ 21 ♈	1 ♏ 19 ♐	1 ♐	1 ♐	1 ♉	1 ♐ 19 ♑	1 ♊	1 ♑
FEB	1 ♓ 13 ♈	1 ♏ 18 ♐	1 ♈	1 ♐	1 ♈ 5 ♉	1 ♐ 9 ♑	1 ♉ 22 ♊	1 ♑ 28 ♒	1 ♊	1 ♑ 6 ♒
MAR	1 ♈ 25 ♉	1 ♐	1 ♈ 4 ♉	1 ♐ 6 ♑	1 ♉ 24 ♊	1 ♑ 23 ♒	1 ♊	1 ♒	1 ♊ 10 ♋	1 ♒ 17 ♓
APR	1 ♉	1 ♐	1 ♉ 16 ♊	1 ♑ ♒	1 ♊	1 ♒	1 ♊ 17 ♋	1 ♒ 7 ♓	1 ♋	1 ♓ 24 ♈
MAY	1 ♉ 6 ♊	1 ♐	1 ♊ 30 ♋	1 ♒	1 ♊ 9 ♋	1 ♒ 3 ♓	1 ♋	1 ♓ 16 ♈	1 ♋ 13 ♌	1 ♈
JUN	1 ♊ 18 ♋	1 ♐	1 ♋	1 ♒ 24 ♓	1 ♋ 26 ♌	1 ♓ 15 ♈	1 ♋ 6 ♌	1 ♈ 26 ♉	1 ♌	1 ♈ 3 ♉
JUL	1 ♋	1 ♐	1 ♋ 16 ♌	1 ♓	1 ♌	1 ♈	1 ♌ 25 ♍	1 ♉	1 ♌ 4 ♍	1 ♉ 14 ♊
AUG	1 ♋ 3 ♌	1 ♐	1 ♌	1 ♓ 24 ♒	1 ♌ 12 ♍	1 ♉	1 ♍	1 ♉ 9 ♊	1 ♍ 21 ♎	1 ♊ 28 ♋
SEP	1 ♌ 19 ♍	1 ♐ 13 ♑	1 ♍	1 ♒	1 ♍ 28 ♎	1 ♉	1 ♍ 10 ♎	1 ♊	1 ♎	1 ♋
OCT	1 ♍	1 ♑ 30 ♒	1 ♍ 18 ♎	1 ♒ 19 ♓	1 ♎	1 ♉	1 ♎ 26 ♏	1 ♊ 3 ♋	1 ♎ 6 ♏	1 ♋ 20 ♌
NOV	1 ♍ 6 ♎	1 ♒	1 ♎	1 ♓	1 ♎ 13 ♏	1 ♉	1 ♏	1 ♋	1 ♏ 18 ♐	1 ♌
DEC	1 ♎ 26 ♏	1 ♒ 11 ♓	1 ♎ 4 ♏	1 ♓ 19 ♈	1 ♏ 28 ♐	1 ♉	1 ♏ 8 ♐	1 ♋ 20 ♊	1 ♐ 29 ♑	1 ♌

♂	1931	1932	1933	1934	1935	1936	1937	1938	1939	1940
JAN	1 ♌	1 ♑ 18 ♒	1 ♍	1 ♒	1 ♎	1 ♒ 14 ♓	1 ♎ 5 ♏	1 ♓ 30 ♈	1 ♏ 29 ♐	1 ♓ 4 ♈
FEB	1 ♌ 16 ♋	1 ♒ 25 ♓	1 ♍	1 ♒ 4 ♓	1 ♎ 22 ♏	1 ♓ 22 ♈	1 ♏	1 ♈	1 ♐	1 ♈ 17 ♉
MAR	1 ♋ 30 ♌	1 ♓	1 ♍	1 ♓ 14 ♈	1 ♎	1 ♈	1 ♏ 13 ♐	1 ♈ 12 ♉	1 ♐ 21 ♑	1 ♉
APR	1 ♌	1 ♓ 3 ♈	1 ♍	1 ♈ 22 ♉	1 ♎	1 ♉	1 ♐	1 ♉ 23 ♊	1 ♑	1 ♊
MAY	1 ♌	1 ♈ 12 ♉	1 ♍	1 ♉	1 ♎	1 ♉ 13 ♊	1 ♐ 14 ♏	1 ♊	1 ♑ 25 ♒	1 ♊ 17 ♋
JUN	1 ♌ 10 ♍	1 ♉ 22 ♊	1 ♍	1 ♉ 2 ♊	1 ♎	1 ♊ 25 ♋	1 ♏	1 ♊ 7 ♋	1 ♒	1 ♋
JUL	1 ♍	1 ♊	1 ♍ 6 ♎	1 ♊ 15 ♋	1 ♎ 29 ♏	1 ♋	1 ♏	1 ♋ 22 ♌	1 ♒ 21 ♑	1 ♋ 3 ♌
AUG	1 ♎	1 ♊ 4 ♋	1 ♎ 26 ♏	1 ♋ 30 ♌	1 ♏	1 ♋ 10 ♌	1 ♏ 8 ♐	1 ♌	1 ♑	1 ♌ 19 ♍
SEP	1 ♎ 17 ♏	1 ♋ 20 ♌	1 ♏	1 ♌	1 ♏ 16 ♐	1 ♌ 26 ♍	1 ♐ 30 ♑	1 ♌ 7 ♍	1 ♑ 24 ♒	1 ♍
OCT	1 ♏ 30 ♐	1 ♌	1 ♏ 9 ♐	1 ♌ 18 ♍	1 ♐ 28 ♑	1 ♍	1 ♑	1 ♍ 25 ♎	1 ♒	1 ♍ 5 ♎
NOV	1 ♐	1 ♌ 13 ♍	1 ♐ 19 ♑	1 ♍	1 ♑	1 ♍ 14 ♎	1 ♑ 11 ♒	1 ♎	1 ♎ 19 ♓	1 ♎ 20 ♏
DEC	1 ♐ 10 ♑	1 ♍	1 ♐ 28 ♑	1 ♍ 11 ♎	1 ♑ 7 ♒	1 ♎	1 ♒ 21 ♓	1 ♎ 11 ♏	1 ♓	1 ♏

MARS TABLES

1941–1950

♂	1941	1942	1943	1944	1945	1946	1947	1948	1949	1950
JAN	1 ♏, 4 ♐	1 ♈, 11 ♉	1 ♐, 26 ♑	1 ♊	1 ♐, 5 ♑	1 ♋	1 ♑, 25 ♒	1 ♍	1 ♑, 4 ♒	1 ♎
FEB	1 ♐, 17 ♑	1 ♉	1 ♑	1 ♊	1 ♑, 14 ♒	1 ♋	1 ♒	1 ♍, 12 ♌	1 ♒, 11 ♓	1 ♎
MAR	1 ♑	1 ♉, 7 ♊	1 ♑, 8 ♒	1 ♊, 29 ♋	1 ♒, 25 ♓	1 ♋	1 ♒, 4 ♓	1 ♌	1 ♓, 21 ♈	1 ♎, 28 ♍
APR	1 ♑, 2 ♒	1 ♊, 26 ♋	1 ♒, 17 ♓	1 ♋	1 ♓	1 ♋, 22 ♌	1 ♓, 11 ♈	1 ♌	1 ♈, 30 ♉	1 ♍
MAY	1 ♒, 16 ♓	1 ♋	1 ♓, 27 ♈	1 ♋, 22 ♌	1 ♓, 3 ♈	1 ♌	1 ♈, 21 ♉	1 ♌, 18 ♍	1 ♉	1 ♍
JUN	1 ♓	1 ♋, 14 ♌	1 ♈	1 ♌	1 ♈, 11 ♉	1 ♌, 20 ♍	1 ♉	1 ♍	1 ♉, 10 ♊	1 ♍, 11 ♎
JUL	1 ♓, 2 ♈	1 ♌	1 ♈, 7 ♉	1 ♌, 12 ♍	1 ♉, 23 ♊	1 ♍	1 ♊	1 ♍, 17 ♎	1 ♊, 23 ♋	1 ♎
AUG	1 ♈	1 ♍	1 ♉, 23 ♊	1 ♍, 29 ♎	1 ♊	1 ♍, 9 ♎	1 ♊, 13 ♋	1 ♎	1 ♋	1 ♎, 10 ♏
SEP	1 ♈	1 ♍, 17 ♎	1 ♊	1 ♎	1 ♊, 7 ♋	1 ♎, 24 ♏	1 ♋	1 ♎, 3 ♏	1 ♋, 7 ♌	1 ♏, 25 ♐
OCT	1 ♈	1 ♎	1 ♊	1 ♎, 13 ♏	1 ♋	1 ♏	1 ♌	1 ♏, 17 ♐	1 ♌, 27 ♍	1 ♐
NOV	1 ♈	1 ♎, 2 ♏	1 ♊	1 ♏, 25 ♐	1 ♋, 11 ♌	1 ♏, 7 ♐	1 ♌	1 ♐, 26 ♑	1 ♍	1 ♐, 6 ♑
DEC	1 ♈	1 ♏, 15 ♐	1 ♊	1 ♐	1 ♌, 26 ♋	1 ♐, 17 ♑	1 ♍	1 ♑	1 ♍, 26 ♎	1 ♑, 15 ♒

1951–1960

♂	1951	1952	1953	1954	1955	1956	1957	1958	1959	1960
JAN	1 ♒, 22 ♓	1 ♎, 20 ♏	1 ♓	1 ♏	1 ♓, 15 ♈	1 ♏, 14 ♐	1 ♐, 28 ♑	1 ♐	1 ♉	1 ♐, 14 ♑
FEB	1 ♓	1 ♏	1 ♓, 8 ♈	1 ♏, 9 ♐	1 ♈, 26 ♉	1 ♐, 28 ♑	1 ♉	1 ♐, 3 ♑	1 ♉, 10 ♊	1 ♑, 23 ♒
MAR	1 ♓, 2 ♈	1 ♏	1 ♈, 20 ♉	1 ♐	1 ♉	1 ♑	1 ♉, 17 ♊	1 ♑, 17 ♒	1 ♊	1 ♒
APR	1 ♈, 10 ♉	1 ♏	1 ♉	1 ♐, 12 ♑	1 ♉, 10 ♊	1 ♑, 14 ♒	1 ♊	1 ♒, 27 ♓	1 ♊, 10 ♋	1 ♒, 2 ♓
MAY	1 ♉, 21 ♊	1 ♏	1 ♊	1 ♑	1 ♊, 26 ♋	1 ♒	1 ♊, 4 ♋	1 ♓	1 ♋	1 ♓, 11 ♈
JUN	1 ♊	1 ♏	1 ♊, 14 ♋	1 ♑	1 ♋	1 ♒, 3 ♓	1 ♋, 21 ♌	1 ♓, 7 ♈	1 ♋, 2 ♌	1 ♈, 20 ♉
JUL	1 ♊, 3 ♋	1 ♏	1 ♋, 29 ♌	1 ♑, 3 ♒	1 ♋, 11 ♌	1 ♓	1 ♌	1 ♈, 21 ♉	1 ♌, 20 ♍	1 ♉
AUG	1 ♋, 18 ♌	1 ♏, 27 ♐	1 ♌	1 ♒, 24 ♓	1 ♌, 27 ♍	1 ♓	1 ♌, 8 ♍	1 ♉	1 ♍	1 ♉, 2 ♊
SEP	1 ♌	1 ♐	1 ♌, 14 ♍	1 ♑	1 ♍	1 ♓	1 ♍, 24 ♎	1 ♉, 21 ♊	1 ♍, 5 ♎	1 ♊, 21 ♋
OCT	1 ♌, 5 ♍	1 ♐, 12 ♑	1 ♍	1 ♑, 21 ♒	1 ♍, 13 ♎	1 ♓	1 ♎	1 ♊, 29 ♉	1 ♎, 21 ♏	1 ♋
NOV	1 ♍, 24 ♎	1 ♑, 21 ♒	1 ♎	1 ♒	1 ♎, 29 ♏	1 ♓	1 ♎, 8 ♏	1 ♉	1 ♏	1 ♋
DEC	1 ♎	1 ♒, 30 ♓	1 ♎, 20 ♏	1 ♒, 4 ♓	1 ♏	1 ♓, 6 ♈	1 ♏, 23 ♐	1 ♉	1 ♏, 3 ♐	1 ♋

– MARS TABLES –

♂	1961	1962	1963	1964	1965	1966	1967	1968	1969	1970
JAN	1 ♋	1 ♑	1 ♌	1 ♑ 13 ♒	1 ♍	1 ♒ 30 ♓	1 ♎	1 ♒ 9 ♓	1 ♏	1 ♓ 24 ♈
FEB	1 ♋ 5 ♊ 7 ♋	1 ♑ 2 ♒	1 ♌	1 ♒ 20 ♓	1 ♍	1 ♓	1 ♎ ♏	1 ♓ 12 ♈	1 ♏ 25 ♐	1 ♈
MAR	1 ♋	1 ♒ 12 ♓	1 ♌	1 ♓ 29 ♈	1 ♍	1 ♓ 9 ♈	1 ♏ 31 ♎	1 ♈ 28 ♉	1 ♐	1 ♈ 7 ♉
APR	1 ♋	1 ♓ 19 ♈	1 ♌	1 ♈	1 ♍	1 ♈ 17 ♉	1 ♎	1 ♉	1 ♐	1 ♉ 18 ♊
MAY	1 ♋ 6 ♌	1 ♈ 28 ♉	1 ♌	1 ♈ 7 ♉	1 ♍	1 ♉ 28 ♊	1 ♎	1 ♉ 8 ♊	1 ♐	1 ♊
JUN	1 ♌ 28 ♍	1 ♉	1 ♌ 3 ♍	1 ♉ 17 ♊	1 ♍ 29 ♎	1 ♊	1 ♎	1 ♊ 21 ♋	1 ♐	1 ♊ 2 ♋
JUL	1 ♍	1 ♉ 9 ♊	1 ♍ 27 ♎	1 ♊ 30 ♋	1 ♎	1 ♊ 11 ♋	1 ♎ 19 ♏	1 ♋	1 ♐	1 ♋ 18 ♌
AUG	1 ♍ 17 ♎	1 ♊ 22 ♋	1 ♎	1 ♋	1 ♎ 20 ♏	1 ♋ 25 ♌	1 ♏	1 ♋ 5 ♌	1 ♐	1 ♌
SEP	1 ♎	1 ♋	1 ♎ 12 ♏	1 ♋ 15 ♌	1 ♏	1 ♌	1 ♏ 10 ♐	1 ♌ 21 ♍	1 ♐ 21 ♑	1 ♌ 3 ♍
OCT	1 ♎ 2 ♏	1 ♋ 11 ♌	1 ♏ 25 ♐	1 ♌	1 ♏ 4 ♐	1 ♌ 12 ♍	1 ♐ 23 ♑	1 ♍	1 ♑	1 ♍ 20 ♎
NOV	1 ♏ 13 ♐	1 ♌	1 ♐	1 ♌ 6 ♍	1 ♐ 14 ♑	1 ♍	1 ♑	1 ♍ 9 ♎	1 ♑ 4 ♒	1 ♎
DEC	1 ♐ 24 ♑	1 ♌	1 ♐ 5 ♑	1 ♍	1 ♑ 23 ♒	1 ♍ 4 ♎	1 ♑ 2 ♒	1 ♎ 30 ♏	1 ♒ 15 ♓	1 ♎ 6 ♏

♂	1971	1972	1973	1974	1975	1976	1977	1978	1979	1980
JAN	1 ♏ 23 ♐	1 ♈	1 ♐	1 ♉	1 ♐ 21 ♑	1 ♊	1 ♑	1 ♋ 26 ♌	1 ♑ 21 ♒	1 ♍
FEB	1 ♐	1 ♈ 10 ♉	1 ♐ 12 ♑	1 ♉ 27 ♊	1 ♑	1 ♊	1 ♑ 9 ♒	1 ♌	1 ♒ 28 ♓	1 ♍
MAR	1 ♐ 12 ♑	1 ♉ 27 ♊	1 ♑ 27 ♒	1 ♊	1 ♑ 3 ♒	1 ♊ 18 ♋	1 ♒ 20 ♓	1 ♌	1 ♓	1 ♍ 12 ♌
APR	1 ♑	1 ♊	1 ♒	1 ♊ 20 ♋	1 ♒ 11 ♓	1 ♋	1 ♓ 28 ♈	1 ♋ 11 ♌	1 ♓ 7 ♈	1 ♌
MAY	1 ♑ 3 ♒	1 ♊ 12 ♋	1 ♒ 8 ♓	1 ♋	1 ♓ 21 ♈	1 ♋ 16 ♌	1 ♈	1 ♌	1 ♈ 16 ♉	1 ♌ 4 ♍
JUN	1 ♒	1 ♋ 28 ♌	1 ♓ 21 ♈	1 ♋ 9 ♌	1 ♈	1 ♌	1 ♈ 6 ♉	1 ♌ 14 ♍	1 ♉ 26 ♊	1 ♍
JUL	1 ♒	1 ♌	1 ♈	1 ♌ 27 ♍	1 ♉	1 ♌ 7 ♍	1 ♉ 18 ♊	1 ♍	1 ♊	1 ♍ 11 ♎
AUG	1 ♒	1 ♌ 15 ♍	1 ♈ 12 ♉	1 ♍	1 ♉ 14 ♊	1 ♍ 24 ♎	1 ♊	1 ♍ 4 ♎	1 ♊ 8 ♋	1 ♎ 29 ♏
SEP	1 ♒	1 ♍	1 ♉	1 ♍ 12 ♎	1 ♊	1 ♎	1 ♊	1 ♎ 20 ♏	1 ♋ 25 ♌	1 ♏
OCT	1 ♒	1 ♎	1 ♉ 30 ♈	1 ♎ 28 ♏	1 ♊ 17 ♋	1 ♎ 9 ♏	1 ♎ 27 ♏	1 ♏	1 ♌	1 ♏ 12 ♐
NOV	1 ♒ 6 ♓	1 ♎ 15 ♏	1 ♈	1 ♏	1 ♋ 26 ♊	1 ♏ 21 ♐	1 ♏	1 ♏ 2 ♐	1 ♌ 20 ♍	1 ♐ 22 ♑
DEC	1 ♓ 26 ♈	1 ♏ 30 ♐	1 ♈ 24 ♉	1 ♏ 11 ♐	1 ♊	1 ♐	1 ♌	1 ♐ 13 ♑	1 ♍	1 ♑ 31 ♒

MARS TABLES

♂	1981	1982	1983	1984	1985	1986	1987	1988	1989	1990
JAN	1 ♒	1 ♎	1 ♒ 17 ♓	1 ♎ 11 ♏	1 ♓	1 ♏	1 ♓ 8 ♈	1 ♏ 9 ♐	1 ♈ 19 ♉	1 ♐ 30 ♑
FEB	1 ♒ 7 ♓	1 ♎	1 ♓ 25 ♈	1 ♏	1 ♓ 3 ♈	1 ♏ 2 ♐	1 ♈ 21 ♉	1 ♐ 22 ♑	1 ♉	1 ♑
MAR	1 ♓ 17 ♈	1 ♎	1 ♈	1 ♏	1 ♈ 15 ♉	1 ♐ 28 ♑	1 ♉	1 ♑	1 ♉ 11 ♊	1 ♑ 12 ♒
APR	1 ♈ 25 ♉	1 ♎	1 ♈ 5 ♉	1 ♏	1 ♉ 26 ♊	1 ♑	1 ♉ 6 ♊	1 ♑ 7 ♒	1 ♊ 29 ♋	1 ♒ 21 ♓
MAY	1 ♉	1 ♎	1 ♉ 17 ♊	1 ♏	1 ♊	1 ♑	1 ♊ 21 ♋	1 ♒ 22 ♓	1 ♋	1 ♓ 31 ♈
JUN	1 ♉ 5 ♊	1 ♎	1 ♊ 29 ♋	1 ♏	1 ♊ 9 ♋	1 ♑	1 ♋	1 ♓	1 ♋ 17 ♌	1 ♈
JUL	1 ♊ 18 ♋	1 ♎	1 ♋	1 ♏	1 ♋ 25 ♌	1 ♑	1 ♋ 7 ♌	1 ♓ 14 ♈	1 ♌	1 ♈ 13 ♉
AUG	1 ♋	1 ♎ 3 ♏	1 ♋ 14 ♌	1 ♏ 18 ♐	1 ♌	1 ♑	1 ♌ 23 ♍	1 ♈	1 ♌ 3 ♍	1 ♉ 31 ♊
SEP	1 ♋ 2 ♌	1 ♏ 20 ♐	1 ♌ 30 ♍	1 ♐	1 ♌ 10 ♍	1 ♑	1 ♍	1 ♈	1 ♍ 20 ♎	1 ♊
OCT	1 ♌ 21 ♍	1 ♐	1 ♍	1 ♐ 5 ♑	1 ♍ 28 ♎	1 ♑ 9 ♒	1 ♍ 9 ♎	1 ♈ 24 ♓	1 ♎	1 ♊
NOV	1 ♍	1 ♑	1 ♍ 18 ♎	1 ♑ 16 ♒	1 ♎	1 ♒ 26 ♓	1 ♎ 24 ♏	1 ♓ 2 ♈	1 ♎ 4 ♏	1 ♊
DEC	1 ♍ 16 ♎	1 ♑ 10 ♒	1 ♎	1 ♒ 25 ♓	1 ♎ 15 ♏	1 ♓	1 ♏	1 ♈	1 ♏ 18 ♐	1 ♊ 14 ♉

♂	1991	1992	1993	1994	1995	1996	1997	1998	1999	2000
JAN	1 ♉ 21 ♊	1 ♐ 9 ♑	1 ♋	1 ♑ 28 ♒	1 ♍ 23 ♌	1 ♐ 9 ♑	1 ♍ 3 ♎	1 ♒ 25 ♓	1 ♎ 26 ♏	1 ♒ 4 ♓
FEB	1 ♊	1 ♑ 18 ♒	1 ♋	1 ♒	1 ♌	1 ♑ 15 ♒	1 ♎	1 ♓	1 ♏	1 ♓ 12 ♈
MAR	1 ♊	1 ♒ 28 ♓	1 ♋	1 ♒ 7 ♓	1 ♌	1 ♒ 25 ♓	1 ♎ 9 ♍	1 ♓ 5 ♈	1 ♏	1 ♈ 23 ♉
APR	1 ♊ 3 ♋	1 ♓	1 ♋ 28 ♌	1 ♓ 15 ♈	1 ♌	1 ♈	1 ♍	1 ♈ 13 ♉	1 ♏	1 ♉
MAY	1 ♋ 27 ♌	1 ♓ 6 ♈	1 ♌	1 ♈ 24 ♉	1 ♌ 26 ♍	1 ♈ 3 ♉	1 ♍	1 ♉ 24 ♊	1 ♏ 6 ♎	1 ♉ 4 ♊
JUN	1 ♌	1 ♈ 15 ♉	1 ♌ 23 ♍	1 ♉	1 ♍	1 ♉ 12 ♊	1 ♍ 19 ♎	1 ♊	1 ♎	1 ♊ 16 ♋
JUL	1 ♌ 16 ♍	1 ♉ 27 ♊	1 ♍	1 ♉ 4 ♊	1 ♍ 21 ♎	1 ♊ 26 ♋	1 ♎	1 ♊ 6 ♋	1 ♎ 5 ♏	1 ♋
AUG	1 ♍	1 ♊	1 ♍ 12 ♎	1 ♊ 17 ♋	1 ♎	1 ♋	1 ♎ 14 ♏	1 ♋ 21 ♌	1 ♏	1 ♌
SEP	1 ♎	1 ♊ 12 ♋	1 ♎ 27 ♏	1 ♋	1 ♎ 7 ♏	1 ♋ 10 ♌	1 ♏ 29 ♐	1 ♌	1 ♏ 3 ♐	1 ♌ 17 ♍
OCT	1 ♎ 17 ♏	1 ♋	1 ♏	1 ♋ 5 ♌	1 ♏ 21 ♐	1 ♌ 30 ♍	1 ♐	1 ♌ 7 ♍	1 ♐ 17 ♑	1 ♍
NOV	1 ♏ 29 ♐	1 ♋	1 ♏ 9 ♐	1 ♌	1 ♐	1 ♍	1 ♐ 9 ♑	1 ♍ 27 ♎	1 ♑ 26 ♒	1 ♍ 4 ♎
DEC	1 ♐	1 ♋	1 ♐ 20 ♑	1 ♌ 12 ♍	1 ♑	1 ♍	1 ♑ 18 ♒	1 ♎	1 ♒	1 ♎ 23 ♏